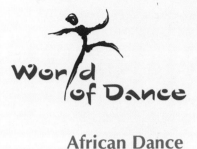

World of Dance

African Dance
Asian Dance
Ballet
European Dance
Middle Eastern Dance
Modern Dance

World of Dance

Modern Dance

Janet Anderson

CHELSEA HOUSE
PUBLISHERS
A Haights Cross Communications Company
Philadelphia

Frontispiece: A dancer in the Alwin Nikolais Ballet. In the 1950s, choreographer Alwin Nikolais experimented with elements such as lighting and costumes while creating dances with no plot, calling his pieces "dance theater."

CHELSEA HOUSE PUBLISHERS

VP, New Product Development Sally Cheney
Director of Production Kim Shinners
Creative Manager Takeshi Takahashi
Manufacturing Manager Diann Grasse

Staff for MODERN DANCE

Editor Ben Kim
Production Assistant Megan Emery
Photo Editor Sarah Bloom
Series & Cover Designer Terry Mallon
Layout 21st Century Publishing and Communications, Inc.

A Haights Cross Communications ◀ Company

www.chelseahouse.com

First Printing

1 3 5 7 9 8 6 4 2

Library of Congress Cataloging-in-Publication Data

Anderson, Janet, 1952–
    Modern dance/by Janet Anderson.
        p. cm. — (World of dance)
Includes index.
Contents: The precursors—Denishawn—Historic dance—The reformers and post-modern dance—Fusion—A modern dance class.
    ISBN 0-7910-7644-X Hardcover   0-7910-7774-8 (PB)
    1. Modern dance—Juvenile literature. 2. Modern dance—History—Juvenile literature. [1. Modern dance. 2. Dance.] I. Title. II. Series.
GV1783.A55 2003
792.8—dc21
                                                           2003009478

Table of Contents

Introduction
Elizabeth A. Hanley
Associate Professor of Kinesiology, Penn State University   **6**

Foreword
Jacques D'Amboise
Founder, National Dance Institute   **8**

1.   **The Precursors**   **12**

2.   **Denishawn**   **24**

3.   **The Historic Modern Dance Generation**   **38**

4.   **The Reformers and Post-Modern Dance**   **52**

5.   **Fusion**   **68**

   A Modern Dance Class   **84**

   Glossary   **94**

   Chronology   **96**

   Videography   **98**

   Websites   **101**

   Bibliography   **102**

   Further Reading   **104**

   Notes   **105**

   Index   **107**

Introduction

Elizabeth A. Hanley
Associate Professor of Kinesiology, Penn State University

Dance has existed from time immemorial. It has been an integral part of celebrations and rituals, a means of communication with gods and among humans, and a basic source of enjoyment and beauty.

Dance is a fundamental element of human behavior and has evolved over the years from primitive movement of the earliest civilizations to traditional ethnic or folk styles, to the classical ballet and modern dance genres popular today. The term 'dance' is a broad one and, therefore, is not limited to the genres noted above. In the 21st century, dance includes ballroom, jazz, tap, aerobics, and a myriad of other movement activities.

The richness of cultural traditions observed in the ethnic, or folk, dance genre offers the participant, as well as the spectator, insight into the customs, geography, dress, and religious nature of a particular people. Originally passed on from one generation to the next, many ethnic, or folk, dances continue to evolve as our civilization and society changes. From these quaint beginnings of traditional dance, a new genre emerged as a way to appeal to the upper level of society: ballet. This new form of dance rose quickly in popularity and remains so today. The genre of ethnic, or folk, dance continues to be an important part of ethnic communities throughout the United States, particularly in large cities.

When the era of modern dance emerged as a contrast and a challenge to the rigorously structured world of ballet, it was not readily accepted as an art form. Modern dance was interested in the communication of emotional experiences—through basic movement, through uninhibited movement—not through the academic tradition of ballet masters. Modern dance, however, found its aficionados and is a popular art form today.

No dance form is permanent, definitive, or ultimate. Change occurs but the basic element of dance endures. Dance is for all people. One need only recall that dance needs neither common race nor common language for communication; it has been a universal means of communication forever.

The WORLD OF DANCE series provides a starting point for readers interested in learning about ethnic, or folk, dances of world cultures, as well as the art forms of ballet and modern dance. This series will feature an overview of the development of these dance genres, from an historical perspective to a practical one. Highlighting specific cultures, their dance steps and movements, their customs and traditions, will underscore the importance of these fundamental elements for the reader. Ballet and modern dance, more recent artistic dance genres, are explored in detail as well, giving the reader a comprehensive knowledge of their past, present, and potential future.

The one fact that each reader should remember is that dance has always been, and always will be, a form of communication. This is its legacy to the world.

❖   ❖   ❖

In this volume, Janet S. Anderson will examine the the fascinating journey and development of modern dance—a relatively young art form that began at the turn of the twentieth century. Pioneers such as Loie Fuller, Isadora Duncan and Ruth St. Denis would break from such dance traditions as ballet, but would also have to fight to gain critical acceptance of their artistic expression. Others would expand upon the abstraction and attention to isolated movement, but modern dance would eventually not only reconcile with ballet, but would also incorporate many other dance styles into its palette.

Foreword

Jacques D'Amboise
Founder, National Dance Institute

"In song and dance, man expresses himself as a member of a higher community. He has forgotten how to walk and speak and is on the way into flying into the air, dancing. . . . his very gestures express enchantment."

—Friedrich Nietzsche

On Maria Dancing by Robert Burns

How graceful Maria leads the dance!
She's life itself. I never saw a foot
So nimble and so elegant; it speaks,
And the sweet whispering poetry it makes
Shames the musicians.

In a conversation with Balanchine discussing the definition of dance, we evolved the following description: "Dance is an expression of time and space, using the control of movement and gesture to communicate."

Dance is central to the human being's expression of emotion. Every time we shake someone's hand, lift a glass in a toast, wave goodbye, or applaud a performer . . . we are doing a form of dance. We live in a universe of time and space, and dance is an art form invented by human beings to express and convey emotions. Dance is profound.

There are melodies that, when played, will cause your heart to droop with sadness for no known reason. Or a rousing jig or mazurka will have your foot tapping in an accompanying rhythm, seemingly beyond your control. The emotions, contacted through music, spur the body to react physically. Our bodies have just been programmed to express emotions. We dance for many reasons: for religious rituals from the most ancient times; for dealing with sadness, tearfully swaying and holding hands at

8

wake; for celebrating weddings, joyfully spinning in circles; for entertainment; for dating and mating. How many millions of couples through the ages have said, "We met at a dance"? But most of all, we dance for joy, often exclaiming, "How I love to dance!" Oh, the JOY OF DANCE!!

I was teaching dance at a boarding school for emotionally disturbed children, ages 9 through 16. They were participating with 20 other schools in the National Dance Institute's (NDI) year-round program. The boarding school children had been traumatized in frightening and mind-boggling ways. There were a dozen students in my class, and the average attention span may have been 15 seconds—which made for a raucous bunch. This was a tough class.

One young boy, an 11-year-old, was an exception. He never took his eyes off of me for the 35 minutes of the dance class, and they were blazing blue eyes—electric, set in a chalk white face. His body was slim, trim, superbly proportioned . . . and he stood arrow-straight. His lips were clamped in a rigid, determined line as he learned and executed every dance step with amazing skill. His concentration was intense despite the wild cavorting, noise, and otherwise disruptive behavior supplied by his fellow classmates.

At the end of class I went up to him and said, "Wow, can you dance. You're great! What's your name?"

Those blue eyes didn't blink. Then he parted his ridged lips and bared his teeth in a grimace that may have been a smile. He had a big hole where his front teeth should be. I covered my shock and didn't let it show. Both top and bottom incisors had been worn away by his continual grinding and rubbing of them together. One of the supervisors of the school rushed over to me and said, "Oh, his name is Michael. He's very intelligent but he doesn't speak."

I heard Michael's story from the supervisor. Apparently, when he was a toddler in his playpen, he witnessed his father shooting his mother—then putting the gun to his own head, the father killed himself. It was close to three days before the neighbors broke in to find the dead and swollen bodies of his parents. The dehydrated and starving little boy was stuck in his playpen, sitting in his own filth. The orphaned Michael disappeared into the foster care system, eventually ending up in the boarding school. No one had ever heard him speak.

In the ensuing weeks of dance class, I built and developed choreography for Michael and his classmates. In the spring, they were scheduled to dance in a spectacular NDI show called *The Event of the Year*. At the boarding school, I used Michael as the leader and as a model for the others and began welding all of the kids together, inventing a vigorous and energetic dance to utilize their explosive energy. It took a while, but they were coming together, little by little over the months. And through all that time, the best in the class—the determined and concentrating Michael—never spoke.

That spring, dancers from the 22 different schools with which the NDI had dance programs were scheduled to come together at Madison Square Garden for *The Event of the Year*. There would be over 2,000 dancers, a symphony orchestra, a jazz orchestra, a chorus, Broadway stars, narrators, and Native American Indian drummers. There was scenery that was the length of an entire city block, and visiting guest children from six foreign countries coming to dance with our New York City children. All of these elements had to come together and fit into a spectacular performance, with only one day of rehearsal. The foremost challenge was how to get 2,000 dancing children on stage for the opening number.

At NDI, we have developed a system called "The Runs." First, we divide the stage into a grid with colored lines making the outlines of box shapes, making a mosaic of patterns and shapes on the stage floor. Each outlined box holds a class from one of the schools, which would consist of 15 to 30 children. Then, we add various colored lines as tracks, starting offstage and leading to the boxes. The dancers line up in the wings, hallways, and various holding areas on either side of the stage. At the end of the overture, they burst onto stage, running and leaping and following their colored tracks to their respective boxes, where they explode into the opening dance number.

We had less than three minutes to accomplish "The Runs." It's as if a couple of dozen trains coming from different places and traveling on different tracks all arrived at a station at the same time, safely pulling into their allotted spaces. But even before starting, it would take us almost an hour just to get the dancers lined up in the correct holding areas offstage, ready to make their entrance. We had scheduled one shot to rehearse the opening. It had to work the first time or we would have to repeat everything. That meant going into overtime at a great expense.

I gave the cue to start the number. The orchestra, singers, lights, and stagehands all commenced on cue, and the avalanche of 2,000 children were let loose on their tracks. "The Runs" had begun!

After about a minute, I realized something was wrong. There was a big pileup on stage left and children were colliding into each other and bunching up behind some obstacle. I ran over to discover the source of the problem   Michael and his classmates. He had ignored everything and led the group from his school right up front, as close to the audience as he could get. Inspiring his dancing buddies, they were a crew of leaping, contorting demons—dancing up a storm, but blocking some 600 other dancers trying to get through.

I rushed up to them yelling, "You're in the wrong place! Back up! Back up!"

Michael—with his eyes blazing, mouth open, and legs and arms spinning in dance movements like an eggbeater—yelled out, "Oh, I am so happy! I am so happy! Thank you Jacques! Oh, it's so good! I am so happy!"

I backed off, stunned into silence. I sat down in the first row of the audience to be joined by several of the supervisors, teachers, and chaperones from Michael's school, our mouths open in wonder. The spirit of dance had taken over Michael and his classmates. No one danced better or with more passion in the whole show that night and with Michael leading the way—the JOY OF DANCE at work. (We went into overtime but so what!)

1

The Precursors

"My art is just an effort to express the truth of my being in gesture and movement." [1]

—Isadora Duncan

When visitors to the Paris Exposition of 1900 crowded into the Palais de Danse to gape at exotic Egyptian belly dancers or Turkish whirling dervishes, they did so in a building crowned by a statue of American dancer Loie Fuller. In order to see Fuller herself dance, one had to enter the vine-carved entrance of the little, art nouveau Le Theatre de la Loie Fuller, which was dedicated only to presenting "La Loie" (as she was known in France) and other protégées. Moving in a blur of scarves and draperies which she manipulated with sticks, Fuller transformed herself into flowers, butterflies, and fire, as colored lights projected from her own small electric dynamo played across her swirling figure. The effect was magical,

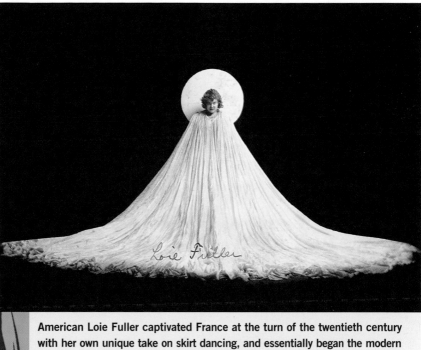

Loie Fuller

American Loie Fuller captivated France at the turn of the twentieth century with her own unique take on skirt dancing, and essentially began the modern dance movement by breaking away from established dance traditions. Her work was immortalized by many artists, and her appearance at the Paris Exposition in 1900 was observed by future modern dance pioneers Isadora Duncan and Ruth St. Denis.

and her audiences gasped and cheered. Using electricity, the most advanced technology of her time, as well as some Yankee ingenuity, Fuller turned her dancing form into a living abstraction.

No one could identify what Fuller was doing, although artists and writers across Europe tried to capture her in motion. She seemed to be the embodiment of the progress that the Exhibition was celebrating—a living, breathing spark of electricity. Nothing was newer than harnessed electric power, and nothing else seemed to hold more promise for the future in 1900. Loie Fuller's whirling form was not new simply because her dance symbolized the larger scientific interests of her era. More than an exotic oddity performing at a world's fair, she was a dancer as radically different and as fueled by new energies as the industrial accomplishments on view at the Exposition.

Fuller was one of the sparks that lit the fire we call modern dance. Two other dancers, Isadora Duncan and Ruth St. Denis, each performing independently of the other, added their own fuel to the early flames. These American women, each following a self-determined method of dancing, were its precursors. Of course, they did not set out to do any such thing, and nor did they call their art "modern dance." All these three women wanted to do was to express themselves as dancers in a highly personal way. Individually and separately, they rejected ballet or theatrical show dancing, the only two concert forms of dance acceptable at the beginning of the twentieth century when their careers flourished. Their dancing is connected only by their will to experiment, for what they performed on stage could not have been more different each from the other.

La Loie literally stumbled into her dance innovation. The oldest of the three dancers, Fuller was born in Illinois in 1869, but hers was not a typical Midwestern childhood. She performed on stages as a child actress and grew up in theater, later moving from Chicago to New York. In 1890, while rehearsing for a play, she kept tripping over the voluminous material of her costume. Eventually, she cleverly placed sticks under her skirt, allowing her the practical accomplishment of being able to lift the fabric off the floor and thus avoid falling down on stage. Quite unexpectedly, she found that moving her draperies in this way glamorously extended the movement of her own body and captivated the audience.

Shifting one's skirts around onstage was an actual genre of dance at that time and was called, appropriately enough, "skirt dancing." The dancer would swing and lift her skirts, perhaps adding some acrobatics, and call it Greek, Oriental, Egyptian, or whatever suited her. It is likely that the then-titillating glimpses of petticoats and even an ankle now and then are what gave the form popularity, for it certainly represented no high artistic aspiration.

There were no ballet companies in America at that time, nor any schools of professional dance. Stage dancing usually meant showgirls performing largely self-taught kicks and turns. Beyond that, personal expression in movement usually referred to the complicated physical culture theories, especially *eurythmics*, a system of harmonious body movements first put forward by Emile Jacques-Dalcroze. At best, this system taught gymnastics in response to music, and at its worst degenerated into pretentious calisthenics programs. Skirt dancing at least provided an outlet for the would-be dance experimenters who used the form in innovative ways.

Fuller perfected her dance illusion touring across America, where her effects were admired as good entertainment. Europeans on the other hand saw her as something more than a touring oddity. Settling in Paris, Fuller found herself celebrated as an artist and a fixture at the famous extravaganza, the Folies Bergère. Loie became the toast of the Parisian art community long before she triumphed at the Paris Exposition.

Artists and writers saw her transform herself into abstract patterns moving on stage, the living expression of artistic ideas sweeping Paris and the world. The ripple of fabric that she sent into the air seemed to mimic the sinuous, decorative move-ment known as Art Nouveau of the late nineteenth and early twentieth centuries. This "New Art" emphasized line, the spiral, and the arabesque. Their long, curving lines were considered to be organic and therefore reflecting nature. Artists employed these curving forms for everything from the famous Paris Metro signs to posters. A Parisian critic noted that when Fuller danced she was "sculptured by the air, the cloth rose and fell, swelled and contracted . . . recalling the fluid lines of Art Nouveau designers . . ."[2]

The Post-Impressionist painter Henri Toulouse-Lautrec, famous for his Art Nouveau-influenced posters of the Paris nightlife he haunted, portrayed Fuller in a lithograph. Upon first glance, she looks like a huge cloud floating in space; only tiny feet under the soaring abstraction reveal this as a woman dancing. Other artists tried to capture Fuller's magic, including sculptor Pierre Roche, whose small bronzes made Fuller look like a beautiful, exotic flower. Even the great sculptor Rodin—whose own work, such as his famous sculpture "The Thinker," celebrated the human body—was interested in sculpting Fuller. Although nothing came of this, he did call her "a woman of genius." [3]

Both Isadora Duncan and Ruth St. Denis saw Fuller perform at the Paris Exposition. While Fuller's extravagant performance was quite far removed from their own emotionally and spiritually conceived dances, they admired her nonetheless. Duncan said of seeing Loie perform, "Before our very eyes she turned to many coloured, shining orchids, to a wavering, flowing sea flower, and at length to a spiral-like lily, all the magic of Merlin, the sorcery of light, colour, flowing form. What an extraordinary genius." [4]

Although she founded a school and staged group productions, Fuller's art was too uniquely her own to survive without her constant attention. When she died, her magic died with her. Admired to the end, famed French author Anatole France contributed the foreword to her autobiography, and Irish poet William Butler Yeats wrote of seeing her: [5]

> When Loie Fuller's Chinese dancers enwound
> A shining web, a floating ribbon of cloth
> It seemed that a dragon of air
> Had fallen among dancers, had whirled them round . . .

Fuller's high theatricality and her submergence of self in costume and light to create a movement effect opened up whole new areas of theater to dancers. The respect she gained

Isadora Duncan believed that movement had to be inspired by emotion, eschewing traditional notions of technique and relying more on personal expression. She would often dance against a simple backdrop and would sometimes even dance in silence without any musical accompaniment.

as an innovator created an artistic climate where other innovators could flourish. The skirt dance was about to disappear,
but Duncan and St. Denis would be burdened with this
characterization before they banished it forever.

Isadora Duncan's story was in some ways similar to
Fuller's. She too became world famous, and was then known
simply by her first name. She was also admired by Rodin,
although his admiration included unwanted amorous
advances. There was, however, nothing accidental about
Duncan's dancing or her career. Encouraged to dance by her
artistic mother, Duncan was a lonely child, growing up in
a family made socially unacceptable because of her father's
financial troubles and her parents' subsequent divorce. Duncan
turned inward, saying later that she began dancing in her
mother's womb. She certainly had complete confidence in her
own intuitive movements from her earliest days. As a teenager,
she and her siblings would teach neighborhood children to
dance. Said Duncan of her earliest instruction, "We called it
a new system of dancing but in reality there was no system.
I followed my fantasy and improvised."[6]

For Duncan, movement sprang out of emotion. This is in
fact the fundamental notion of the Duncan style. The dancer
needs to go into his or her very center and produce a pure
movement in response to specific feeling. This had nothing to
do with technique. There were no positions to learn or steps to
memorize, and Duncan avoided special lighting or stage
effects. "My art," she said, "is just an effort to express the truth
of my being in gesture and movement."[7]

Early on in her life, Duncan focused on the idea of
becoming a serious concert dancer while using her own style
of movement. As a teenager accompanied by her family,
she went first to Chicago and then on to New York looking for
work as a dancer. Without much difficulty, she found jobs in
musical revues, but she felt this was not true to her theory of
dancing. Seeking to express pure emotion through movement,

Duncan looked for a place where she could perform. She was forced to take her serious, introspective solo dances into society ladies' salons, where she was politely applauded. But Duncan wanted recognition as an artist, not as a parlor entertainer. Seeking a more appreciative audience, Duncan and her accommodating family went first to London and then to Paris, where, like Loie Fuller, she found great success and a new home.

Isadora Duncan must have been a sight to behold. Her emotive dance was performed wearing loose tunics (and later, beautifully draped Grecian robes) and she usually danced without shoes of any kind. She performed on bare stages in front of a simple blue backdrop with the accompaniment of highly dramatic classical music—Beethoven and Wagner being particular favorites—or in absolute silence. She looked—as indeed she had intended to—as though she had stepped off an ancient fresco of dancing goddesses. She often paused to tell the audience her views on current events, creating a sense that the entire production was improvised. This however was not true, as her dances were carefully crafted, although changed and modified in any given performance. They are recreated even today by her still dedicated followers.

Duncan was an original who really was touched with genius. Careful reconstructions of her famous dances show us nothing of the power she had individually as a performer. As Agnes de Mille observed, "Her greatest technical contribution—her personal performance—tends to be forgotten because it cannot be copied."[8]

Loie Fuller saw Duncan dance in Paris, and the two dancers admired each other's work. Fuller arranged for Duncan to join a tour to Berlin. The Germans in particular were taken by Isadora's approach to dancing, as they had embraced the movement systems popular at the time, particularly those of Dalcroze's eurythmics. Isadora's more personal, emotion-based theories of dance were not strictly the same as those of Dalcroze and his followers. However, both styles could look the same since each relied on an easily moving, well-balanced body using simple gestures to express emotion. So enthusiastic were the Germans about Duncan's innovative dancing that she chose to establish her first school teaching the Isadora Duncan dance method in Berlin in 1905.

In personal matters however, Duncan had a dramatic and unhappy life. She became a passionate feminist as a result of seeing her mother struggle to support her family while being scorned for her divorce. When Duncan herself had two children of her own, she chose not to marry their father. Her pleasure in her children was short-lived as they drowned in a freakish automobile accident in Paris in 1913 when the car plunged into the River Seine. Duncan sank into despair, and her dances at that time, like "March Slav," reflect this emotional state.

Admiring the Bolshevik revolution in Russia, Duncan defended the newly Communist Soviet Russia, eventually even moving to Russia where she established yet another European dance institute in 1921 in Moscow. She was completely oblivious to critics who labeled her a Communist, even composing dances to be performed at Lenin's funeral. After avoiding the convention of marriage for her entire life, Isadora surprised everyone in 1922 by marrying the young Russian poet Sergey Yesenin, who was 17 years her junior. An impoverished Duncan eventually left Russia in 1924 after her school lost government support and her moody husband had committed suicide.

Tragedies and setbacks however never affected Duncan for long. She returned to France and began giving dance performances again, demonstrating that her charisma was undiminished by age. Her comeback triumph did not last long, unfortunately. A bizarre automobile accident claimed her life in 1927 when she dramatically tossed a scarf around her neck as she got into a sports car. Caught in the wheel spokes, the scarf broke her neck when the car moved forward.

She had more to tell the world, however; her autobiography appeared almost immediately following her death.

Isadora Duncan never set out to be part of a reforming movement in dance. She considered her art to be true dance— genius, in fact—and what everyone else did was simply theatrical silliness. She intellectualized her movements while claiming they sprang from emotions. The notion of dance as expression of inner states of being was Isadora's gift to what became modern dance. This was a very new concept indeed. Certainly no skirt dancer before her ever had made such extravagant claims!

If Isadora turned to emotion as movement's source, her contemporary, Ruth St. Denis, looked to what she called the spirit. Born Ruth Dennis in 1879 in New Jersey, she changed her name in the early years of her career when she danced in musical revues. A producer called her "Saint Dennis" as a way of teasing her about her high-minded and serious approach to dance. She liked the sound of St. Denis, and it was true that for her, dance was a spiritual pursuit. "As I see it," she said, "the deepest lack of Western cultures is any true workable system for teaching a process of integration between soul and body."[9]

Like Fuller and Duncan before her, St. Denis' earliest stage appearances were in popular musical theater. While on tour in 1904, she happened to see a cigarette advertisement with a picture of the Egyptian goddess Isis. This image so captured her imagination that she became determined to create dances in the Oriental manner—that is, a Western notion of Eastern cultures that was more romanticized than authentic. She eventually became receptive to the entire spectrum of spiritual thought that she associated with the Near East and Far East.

St. Denis was a beautiful, mesmerizing performer like Duncan and Fuller, but she was less fussy about where she danced. Although she toured in Europe, St. Denis' professional life unfolded in America, and she actu   ¹ her first major success, *Radha*, with the vaudevill   ɩt in mind. *Radha* was her solo dance, and she portrayed a Hindu temple

Ruth St. Denis often danced in garb invoking images of the Middle East and other exotic cultures, in combination with dance steps borrowed from various disciplines. While her dances and costumes were not necessarily genuinely authentic, her own interpretations were highly imaginative and combined dance styles from various genres.

idol. She was so hypnotizing as she slithered off her temple pedestal to explore the temptations of the senses that it hardly mattered that her steps were a hodge-podge of ballet turns, acrobatics in the eurythmic tradition, and poses that froze the lovely St. Denis into Oriental images directly out of nothing more authentic than her own imagination. No one cared that the set was not the Jain Temple or that the music by Delibes had been composed for a European opera. This formula would be reinvented throughout St. Denis' career as she singly—and eventually with a company—brought the entire world of mysticism and Oriental religious practices as she envisioned it to stages of all sizes across the country.

In 1914, influenced by the enormous success of the ballroom dancers Irene and Vernon Castle (who were then at the height of their fame), St. Denis decided to find a male partner. But she was more interested in the performing tension between male and female partners than ballroom dance. She selected Ted Shawn, a former divinity student, who had trained in ballet for therapeutic reasons. He was a handsome man with a physique that people compared to a Greek god. Spiritually a seeker as well and physically the male equal of her beauty, he was an ideal match for St. Denis. Together they became Denishawn.

Denishawn shifts the story of modern dance away from the precursors. St. Denis and Shawn created more than a dance company—they started a dance school, brought men into dance innovation, and eventually created one of the most important dance festivals in the world. They were innovators who were not uncomfortable creating institutions that would secure a place for modern dance in theater arts. Fuller and Duncan had been worshipped in their lifetimes, but only St. Denis lived long enough to hear herself called the mother of modern dance.

2

Denishawn

"Dance . . . the symbol and language for communicating spiritual truth."

—Ruth St. Denis [10]

When Ruth St. Denis married Ted Shawn in 1914, neither could have imagined the dance legacy their union would produce. At the time, it seemed a straightforward partnership of two attractive dancers who both needed something the other had to give. St. Denis wanted a male dance partner, and Shawn, who had long admired St. Denis' spiritual approach to dance, wanted to learn from her. The two shared long-term dreams of a school and dance communities that would be centered on utopian ideals. Almost immediately, they began a conversation about such goals. If the introspective St. Denis tended to see these possibilities as spiritual directions, the ever-practical Shawn started to implement them almost at once.

Ruth St. Denis and her husband Ted Shawn became known as Denishawn, which also became the name of the dance school St. Denis had started, as well as their touring company. Shawn took on most of the teaching duties, reflecting the more organizational and practical aspects that Shawn brought to their partnership.

Billed as "Ruth St. Denis, assisted by Ted Shawn, with Hilda Beyer" (his dance partner at that time), the two began touring. Not long after they had started working together and just as World War I officially began, they married on August 13, 1914. St. Denis was 36 and Shawn was just 23. Prematurely white-haired, St. Denis was a regal figure, and Shawn, at over six feet tall, made a noble consort. The name "Denishawn" was actually not of their design but rather the result of an enterprising theater owner's promotion, and it stuck, although the company that began with their partnership would continue to be billed as "Ruth St. Denis" until 1921.

Romantic as the combined name sounds, there was a tension between the couple from the start. St. Denis, the dreamer, and Shawn, the realist, were often at odds. Depending on the observer's point of view, Shawn either was St. Denis' perfect complement or someone who used her to further his own ambition. Agnes de Mille, the great dancer-*choreographer* who knew both dancers, observed much later,

> he (Shawn) refers to her as though she were his guru. But she was not his guru, she was his middle-aged wife, famous while he was unknown, sought after while he was passed by, worshipped by dancers while he was tolerated as their equal, envied only as having special and unfair advantages. In short, she was a genuine star while he was a pretender. She was also a woman of genuine convictions; what he had were genuine ambitions.[11]

Others were less unkind. Jane Sherman, a member of the Denishawn troupe who worked closely with the two for years, observed more mildly that, "She supplied the glamour and inspiration, he the organization and teaching drive."[12]

In any event, the 1915 opening of the Ruth St. Denis School of Dancing on a wooded hilltop in Los Angeles was a major milestone—not just in the lives of these two dancers but also in the history of American dance. By the next year, the name was changed to the Denishawn School, thus officially acknowledging the joint nature of their endeavors. For St. Denis, the school was a place of final repose in a lifetime of touring, providing her a base from which to practice and reaffirm her spiritual goals. She had limited interest in teaching, however, and focused her energies primarily on performance. She had been dancing professionally long before achieving real success in 1906's *Radha* when she was 27 years old. The huge success of this "Indian" dance propelled her into years of touring in vaudeville and performing in private engagements.

As St. Denis' repertory had expanded to Egyptian and Japanese themes, she used dancers on an as-needed basis to fill out larger dances. When she had mounted her full-length *Egypta* with a cast of 50 in 1910, the dancers were hired for the tour and the elaborate costumes and sets of this dance-theater piece had to be built for ease in transport. So the establishment of a school with facilities for training dancers as well as for creating and storing sets and costumes was no small gift from a young husband to a revered older wife. The Los Angeles facility was joined later by the addition of a major Denishawn center in New York City and countless branches across the entire United States. Shawn made it possible for his charismatic wife to become universally known and admired as "Miss Ruth," as well as showing the way for future generations to financially support their creative concert work on a foundation of teaching and touring.

The goal of the school was "The eternal quest for truth, the ecstasy of an instant's communication with a divine being, the harmony of rituals, beautifully performed."[13] If Shawn's drive brought the school into being, it was St. Denis' vision that kept Denishawn set on a course of high purpose where spiritual goals would be pursued in partnership with performing. It would be a place where Miss Ruth could hold seminars on Oriental mysticism and religion, at least as it was known in the West at that time. It was a heady infusion of breathing exercises, meditation, Hindu philosophy and even Christian Science practices.

St. Denis did not teach dance, although she instructed on facial expressions and gestures. Shawn and a small teaching staff introduced students to a variety of Oriental dances as well as ballet and general movement exercises, based primarily on the Delsarte method of "natural" movement theory. The school managed to advertise itself as something of a finishing school, which attracted the daughters and sons of the middle class. However, the school's prosperous neighbors, residing in secluded and beautifully landscaped homes nearby, found the undertaking dangerously arty. Every incident, like the young women of Denishawn dashing down the suburban street in bathing suits trying to retrieve the resident peacock, managed to be reported in the newspaper. To this island of serene introspection and emotive movement high in the Los Angeles hills came dancers from all over. Some stayed for a session or two and drifted away, while others became members of the Denishawn touring company. Three of them would eventually split away from Denishawn to form their own companies— thus actually beginning modern dance as we know it.

In 1916, in the second summer of the school's existence, the first of the threesome, Martha Graham, entered the school in spite of Miss Ruth's initial reaction that she was "totally hopeless"[14] and considered to be short, dumpy, and untrained. Doris Humphrey arrived from Chicago in 1917 with the goal of simply teaching dance, and in her case, Miss Ruth approved, saying to her, "You should dance."[15] At about the same time, Charles Weidman arrived from Lincoln, Nebraska, where he had seen Denishawn on tour.

One other key figure in the history of modern dance was also in the group. Louis Horst was Denishawn's musical director from 1915 to 1925 and would go on to accompany, compose for, and collaborate with succeeding generations of modern dance innovators. The impact of this quartet lay in the future; for the next 15 years, their lives would be intertwined with Denishawn and their personal visions would be submerged in its high exoticism.

Unlike Loie Fuller and Isadora Duncan, St. Denis and Shawn were interested in finding an audience in America. To do this, they took the company to the small towns and burgeoning cities of the 48 states. They did not despise the vaudeville circuit as Duncan and Fuller had, nor did they feel that their artistic integrity was in any way threatened. The only truly respectable stage for dance was at the New York Metropolitan Opera House, but opportunities there were very limited and mostly restricted to ballet dancers filling out crowd scenes in opera productions.

To most Americans, vaudeville simply meant a variety show presented in a theater. Small theaters across the United States were built by enterprising owners who created chains while others were individually owned. The term "vaudeville" comes from the French term *vaux-de-ville*, used in France as early as the eighteenth century to describe a theatrical entertainment with a variety of acts. But by the 1880s, vaudeville was universally accepted in the United States as a variety show that could consist of dancers, comedians, singers, acrobats, animal acts, and just about any stage novelty imaginable. When motion pictures began, vaudeville acts often preceded or followed the film presentation. For almost 80 years, vaudeville provided the average American access to entertainment and culture.

Ruth St. Denis had first presented *Radha*, the dance that made her famous, at Worth's Family Theater and Museum. Here she danced six times a day on a program of variety acts in a setting that was shared with displays of pickled animal freaks and between lectures on historical relics which were also on view. So, going from one theater to another as a featured act of a theater chain did not seem all that terrible. St. Denis could also leave the tedious task of bookings or arranging tour logistics to the impresario hiring her troupe.

As the Denishawn company grew in size, augmented continuously by dancers training at its own school, the company's productions became grander. Each program included several St. Denis solos, which might be anything from her famous *Cobras*, in which her multi-jointed arms became serpents, to *Yogi*, just one of her many dance meditations based on Eastern religious practices. St. Denis and Shawn

Denishawn performing in Asian costume. Denishawn performed in many settings that were not necessarily limited to proper stages or dance venues, even appearing on the vaudeville circuit—something Fuller and Duncan had thought of as too low and common for presenting their artistic visions.

began performing in new works that showcased their combined talent in duets ranging from ballroom dance to mystical and exotic creations such as *The Garden of Kama*, a love story between a highborn Indian beauty and a fisherman. The program also included full company dances and usually one or two short "musical visualizations" which St. Denis described as "the scientific translation into bodily action of the rhythmic, melodic, and harmonious structure of musical composition." St. Denis readily said that Isadora Duncan had inspired her to approach music in this way. Through the years, Shawn began to be showcased in solo work as well, and later, his own full-company choreography was performed. Each of these was a short work that could be interspersed throughout a program with other acts.

An opportunity to work on a large scale came to Denishawn in 1916 in the form of an invitation to perform in the Greek Theatre of the University of California at Berkeley. Denishawn was the first dance company so honored. St. Denis used the entire school to create a dance pageant of Egyptian, Greek, and Indian styles, including having the students dye and stencil cloth as well as sew some of the 450 costumes. In addition to the Denishawn students, St. Denis used almost 100 dancers from the Berkeley summer session.

St. Denis' dream of recapturing the spirit of ancient performance was nearly realized in the Berkeley commission. Later in life, she said, "The experience of these rehearsals is among the high points of my career." She mused happily over the long hours of rehearsal with trunks of costumes open in the sunshine and the pleasant sounds of hammering going on backstage where sets and props were being constructed. All the while visitors strolled by watching the preparations. She had felt then as though "The antique world hovered in the radiant sunshine. We could have been in a Greek theater in the ancient land."[16]

Each of the pageant sections portrayed daily life and spiritual pursuits of the three selected civilizations of Egypt, Greece, and India. An actual river of water created along a broad walk at the front of the stage successively represented the Nile, the Styx, and finally the Ganges. One of St. Denis and Shawn's most enduring dance duets, *Toilers of the Soil*, appeared first in the Egyptian section. For *Toilers*, the twosome moved in profile like hieroglyphic stick figures as they went about their daily tasks of plowing, planting, and harvesting. Shawn's head was shaved and he wore a loincloth, while St. Denis was draped in a shapeless, sack-like garment. This dance is one of the very few to survive in film, and while both dancers were over 60 years old at the time it was filmed, Shawn's balletic training and poise still is apparent, as is St. Denis' mesmerizing ability at suggesting character and thought in movement. The pageant would be performed at the Panama California Exposition in San Diego, as well as in Los Angeles and Santa Barbara. Its individual dances, such as *Toilers in the Soil*, would enter into the permanent Denishawn repertory.

Although a huge artistic success, the pageant left Denishawn in debt. As St. Denis said, the only real answer to this problem was "Vaudeville. This contingency always disturbed Ted more than it did me. He sometimes questioned whether this means of freeing ourselves from debt was worth the loss in artistic prestige which he believed accompanied a two-a-day. But to me debt loomed as a greater moral defeat than any hypothetical loss of prestige."[17]

One other avenue of popular work supported Denishawn: the burgeoning movie industry that was then taking root in Los Angeles. The sumptuous, epic nature of Denishawn found its counterpart in the silent movies then being produced by Cecil B. de Mille (whose niece, Agnes de Mille, would become a dancer-choreographer) and D. W. Griffiths. Both virtually invented the oversized screen epic with films like *The Ten Commandments* and *Birth of a Nation*. Many Denishawn dancers and students ended up in motion pictures, including Julianne Johnston, who starred with Douglas Fairbanks in *The Thief of Baghdad*. Silent-screen great Louise Brooks, herself a film icon, was also a Denishawn dancer. D. W. Griffiths actually required his actresses to attend Denishawn classes to learn how to convey emotion through movement. St. Denis choreographed a Babylonian dance for Griffith's huge film *Intolerance*, calling on Denishawn students to appear in it.

Ted Shawn in Native American costume. After returning from service with the Ambulance Corps in World War I, Shawn began experimenting with choreography himself, incorporating elements of American Indian culture in his work.

Touring, however, paid the bills. Following the pageant's success in 1916, the troupe spent the rest of that year and much of 1917 performing on the Orpheum vaudeville circuit. With America's entrance into World War I and Shawn's enlistment in the United States Army Ambulance Corps, St. Denis toured vaudeville on her own once again. When the war ended and Shawn returned, Denishawn was promptly out touring the Pantages vaudeville circuit in 1919. During this time, Shawn himself began experimenting as a choreographer. He took the exploration of American Indian myth and tradition as his personal territory in such dances as *Xochitl*, which gave Martha Graham her first star turn as a feisty Toltec maiden.

Year after year, the dancers were on the road doing "two-a-day" performances on the vaudeville circuit, which one former dancer described as "uninspiring, almost degrading labor."[18] It was not uncommon for Denishawn, even with its high art aspirations, to appear on a program with comedian Fanny Brice as the next act. Denishawn even had the honor of playing New York's Palace, vaudeville's greatest stage, where they were so popular that they were extended for a second week. The high point of their life on the road came in 1925 and 1926 with a prestigious tour throughout the Orient, taking their Western imitations of Eastern religion and myth to the source itself. They visited eight countries, including Japan, China, and India. The tour was a triumph, with Eastern audiences more appreciative of the implied compliment than critical of any irregularities or errors in Denishawn's vision of them. The troupe returned home exhausted only to go back on the road immediately, spending 40 weeks in 1927 and 1928 touring with the Ziegfeld Follies.

By now, the pressure of touring was taking its toll on everyone in the company. Drawn to Denishawn by a desire to perform serious, high art dance, the troupe felt wearied, and sometimes even sullied, by the grueling demands of touring and the often makeshift environments where they performed. Shawn and St. Denis' relationship was strained by this as well. St. Denis was never comfortable as a married woman, resisting the notion of an ordinary life, family, and a home. Meanwhile, Shawn pushed for more control over Denishawn as well as visibility for his own dance works. He also was a fervent pioneer in the effort to lure men back to serious dance after a long period where dancing was considered—especially in the United States —to be something that only women did. St. Denis wanted time to reflect and to recoup, but Shawn, ever full of energy, burst with new ideas for the company. Both partners had flirtations with other people, and there were rumors that Shawn's were with other men, something vehemently denied at a time when homosexuality actually was illegal in much of the United States. Shawn summed up his own view of the situation when he wearily titled one of his books *One Thousand and One Night Stands.*

Martha Graham was the first dancer to defect, but others such as Doris Humphrey and Charles Weidman would follow, going on to become the great founding generation of independent modern dance artists. Less inevitable but perhaps even more damaging was the departure of Louis Horst, Denishawn's musical director. Unlike dancers, who—at least in theory— could easily be replaced within the Denishawn system, Horst's contribution was fundamental to the acts of choreographing and producing. There were no other composer-musicians training in Denishawn workshops.

Agnes de Mille called Graham's departure "the first wound in the flesh of Denishawn,"[19] saying Graham "spurned" Shawn in particular. Graham herself described her leave more prosaically, saying, "Denishawn was preparing for their famous tour of the Orient and we were all excited . . . I was told I looked too Oriental and would not be a true representative of Denishawn."[20] The truth lies somewhere in between. Miss Ruth never liked Graham's dancing, though Shawn encouraged her, even making her a teacher. Graham felt misunderstood and underutilized. She even carried around clippings that said Graham was the only Denishawn dancer to perform with passion and excitement. Each of this threesome had a well-developed ego, and a split was inevitable.

Denishawn sputtered to an end in the early 1930s, a victim of the economic crisis of the Great Depression as well as the

Shawn with Martha Graham. Graham had been with the Denishawn company since 1916 but had never been regarded highly by St. Denis, though Shawn had encouraged her dancing. Eventually Graham was the first dancer to leave Denishawn, ready to hone her own personal dance vision.

internal strains within the company. They had accomplished great things, touring and bringing their artistic yearnings to all America. Men and women began to look at stage dance as a potentially real art form, and a generation of young people was inspired to dance. By 1932, Shawn had struck off on his own, touring with his own Company of Male Dancers. He eventually turned his farm in upstate New York, "Jacob's Pillow," into an important summer dance festival. St. Denis returned to solo performances, usually in a religious setting. The couple parted, and while they never divorced, they lived separately for the rest of their long lives.

Meanwhile on October 28, 1928, Doris Humphrey and Charles Weidman, along with 16 other dancers, made American dance history with the first performance by a modern dance ensemble. This, in combination with Martha Graham's 1926 solo concert, established the idea of modern dance as an art form based on individual movement vocabularies unrelated to the past. Almost every modern dancer performing today can trace his or her own dance lineage back to one of these three Denishawn dancers.

Ruth St. Denis died in 1968, and Ted Shawn in 1970. No one had called their art "modern dance." After Denishawn, dancers as well as painters, musicians, and authors were called modern artists. Denishawn, in its lovely Spanish mansion overlooking Los Angeles, was the cradle of a great theater movement where dancers were taught not only how to move but also to have the confidence to assume the title of artist.

3

The Historic
Modern Dance
Generation

"I feel that the essence of dance is the expression of man—the landscape of his soul. "

—Martha Graham [21]

By the late 1920's, Americans had become accustomed to the idea of "artistic" dance. Denishawn had crisscrossed the country many times as well as making itself newsworthy with its famous Orient tour. Moreover, Isadora Duncan, while reviled in her lifetime as a decadent Communist, inspired young women across America to seek self-expression by putting on Greek tunics and dancing barefoot. Ballet also attracted widespread interest as Anna Pavlova toured the United States, leaving in her wake scores of would-be ballerinas, including Agnes de Mille. Meanwhile, word filtered back from Europe that Russian impresario Serge Diaghilev was presenting dazzling new productions with charismatic dancers like Vaslav Nijinsky. The

Graham's first years out of Denishawn were spent performing as a showgirl in the Greenwich Village Follies. While she had the opportunity to perform solos, she left the Follies in 1925 and joined the Eastman School of Music in Rochester, New York. She left the school after only a year and started to work on her own, but it would be a few years before her vision was fully formed.

latter performed in ballets utilizing innovative collaborators, including composer Igor Stravinsky, artist Pablo Picasso, and choreographer George Balanchine.

This general climate of curiosity about serious dance was new. Martha Graham, Doris Humphrey, and Charles Weidman benefited from it, and were also inspired by it. The decision to leave Denishawn to evolve a personal way of moving might not have happened in a less supportive cultural climate. Each dancer had come of age professionally in the exuberant post-World War I era when skirts went up, jazz and nightclubs thrived, movie palaces appeared across the country, and the automobile made Americans increasingly mobile. It was a time of high confidence and experimentation. Graham, Humphrey, and Weidman were uninterested in conquering Europe or in the great reforms sweeping ballet; they sought to find movement that represented American energy.

The dancers who embarked on this exciting artistic journey could not know that within a few years of their first solo concerts, this environment of high excitement and encouragement of the arts would literally disappear. In 1929, the crash of the stock market precipitated a worldwide economic depression. Bread-lines, hobos, and striking workers replaced the high-living flappers and their tuxedoed admirers. "Brother, Can You Spare a Dime?" was the song on everyone's lips. Abroad, Hitler seized power in Germany as did Mussolini in Italy, and civil war broke out in Spain. The confident, affluent 1920s disappeared into the fearful, impoverished Depression era of the 1930s. Inevitably, the change was reflected in the arts.

Martha Graham did not immediately take to the stage and become the great lady of American modern dance. She had a long period of trial and error before entering her great era of sustained choreographic invention in her 40s. When she first left Denishawn, she happily performed for two years in the Greenwich Village Follies, becoming something of a Broadway star where "each night one of my solos," she exulted, "would stop the show."[22] Restless and unsatisfied with the life of a showgirl, even a very popular one, Graham left the Follies in 1925 in order, as she stated, "to create my own dances, on my own body."

Although Graham remained a loner all her life, she had a knack for finding people who saw something special in her and were willing to lend her substantial assistance. This happened when she had first applied at Denishawn and been turned away by Miss Ruth only to have Ted Shawn step in. He recognized Martha's sheer determination and decided to encourage her drive and determination. Although the relationship between Shawn and Graham ended in disillusionment, each acknowledged the role Shawn had played in Martha's Denishawn career. Shawn went so far as to say, "I trained her. Ruth didn't and wouldn't. There'd be no Martha Graham without me."[23] Graham however had a different take on her Denishawn experience, saying, "I worshipped everything about Miss Ruth—how she walked, how she danced. Miss Ruth was everything to me, but I got stuck with Ted who really was something of a dud."[24]

Her Broadway exit came about when Rouben Mamoulian, a Russian-born theatrical director, invited her to act as co-director of the newly established dance department at Eastman School of Music in Rochester, New York. George Eastman, whose invention of the Kodak camera in 1888 had made him wealthy enough to turn to philanthropy, had brought in Mamoulian to direct his School of Music. Mamoulian surprised everyone by insisting on including a dance department. "Dance," he declared, "is the foundation of the theater."[25] Mamoulian had seen Graham perform on Broadway and thought her a gifted and an unusual personality—and, like himself, a very idiosyncratic talent.

Louis Horst, who had spent time in Vienna after leaving Denishawn as its musical director, joined Graham at Eastman. Others would regard such artistic encouragement and collaboration as wonderful, but Graham, who did not have a spirit suited to institutions with or without congenial colleagues, left after one year.

Using three Eastman students, Graham gave her first

independent dance concert in New York City at the Forty-Eighth Street Theater on April 18, 1926—but it was not the debut that would have critics hailing her as a genius. Alas, even some of the titles of these first dances show her still locked into a Denishawn approach to movement and programming: *Three Gopi Maidens, Florentine Madonna,* and *Clair de Lune.* Any of these would have been appropriate for one of Miss Ruth's dance dramas or music visualizations. The newspapers remarked that the work was merely "pretty" and "graceful,"[26] and Graham herself conceded her first dances were "influenced by Denishawn."[27]

Graham continued to experiment with movement, focusing on a new way for the dancer to breathe that she called "a contraction and a release"—that is, not only to breathe involuntarily, but also to exaggerate the sharp intake of breath and its explosive expulsion. Even today when a Graham-trained dancer performs this torso-based movement, the viewer can see the body pull back at its center and then expand outward—like being socked in the stomach. Graham based her dances not on simple counts as most choreographers do, but on breath-counts: short, fast breath quickly expelled for anger, and longer, slower breath counts for quieter moods. Used this way, she invited the audience, instinctively breathing the same rhythm, to be pulled emotionally into the performance as well.[28]

Most stage dance technique before Graham elongated the body and moved it upward into space, as did ballet. Graham on the other hand celebrated the floor and the earth—sitting on it, falling on it, and touching it. Deliberately violating ballet's classical technique of pointing the foot and creating a line of the leg from thigh to toe, she danced flat-footed and with bare (and often flexed) feet. These innovations were not new—they had all been employed at Denishawn—but that company used them in the service of exoticism. Graham used these techniques without glamorous trappings. She did not disguise the effort that went into her movements—she sweated. She would not leap; she pounced. When she kicked her leg in the air, the audience saw a dirty foot. It was not pretty, and Graham acknowledged that "In many ways I showed onstage what most people came to the theatre to avoid."[29]

It would take years for Martha Graham's technique to mature, but all the elements were in place by the late 1920s and early 1930s. In 1927, she showed a solo dance called *Revolt* which was about man's injustice to man. It was definitely not a Denishawn or ballet topic. Reviewers called this work "stark" and even "ugly." Graham had found her idiom, and from this point she experimented with movement that made a statement. She wanted technique to service her ideas rather than demonstrate dance virtuosity. It was not that she deliberately wanted to antagonize audiences, "but I'd rather they disliked me than be apathetic, because that is the kiss of death," observed Graham.[30]

In 1929, she presented *Heretic*, her first concert dance for a company of dancers. Wearing a simple, long white jersey dress, Graham confronted 12 women in identical long, black dresses who became, in her words, "a wall of defiance that I could not break."[31] A Breton song played and then stopped; at this moment of silence, the women in black reformed into another group. Explained Graham, "I was the heretic desperately trying to force myself free of the darkness of my oppressors."[32] She herself was a heretic in the world of dance, challenging old conceptions of dance and facing similar opposition. People either loved her boldness or hated it.

The next year, she created and performed *Lamentation*, a solo performed seated while she stretched and moved inside a long tube of jersey material—"to indicate," Graham said, "the tragedy that obsesses the body, the ability to stretch inside your own skin, to witness and test the perimeter and boundaries of grief . . . "[33] Martha Graham had found her genius.

Martha Graham was not the only former Denishawn dancer performing new work on the concert stage. Doris

Doris Humphrey and Charles Weidman were two dancers who had also left Denishawn to start their own company, Humphrey-Weidman. Humphrey continued to teach and choreograph after arthritis prevented her from performing, and composed dances to be performed in silence or to minimal music or sounds.

Humphrey and Charles Weidman left Denishawn far less dramatically than had Graham. From the beginning, their company, known as Humphrey-Weidman, was composed of both men and women; Graham's company, in contrast, was all-female for its first 15 years. While both Humphrey and Weidman were powerful soloists, their work was conceived primarily for a group to perform. Individually, Humphrey was an exquisite dancer performing "like a nymph" in airy, light, delicate movements, in direct contrast to Graham's earthbound ficrceness.[34] Weidman was that rare thing in modern dance— a humorist and mime, someone whose most celebrated dances made people laugh. Neither had the immense personality of Graham, her glamour, nor her occasionally irritating highhandedness.

Humphrey had come to Denishawn after teaching dance in Chicago, and it was St. Denis who saw her talent and urged her to perform. To the end of her days, Humphrey remained at heart a natural teacher, leaving behind a legacy of talented dancers. One of these, José Limón, would be at the forefront of the next modern generation. She never was interested solely in creating new dances but equally in developing a dance language that facilitated movement composition.

If Martha Graham wanted to explore her interior life, Doris Humphrey was much more interested in abstract questions about the nature of movement. "My entire technique," said Humphrey, "consists of the development of the process of falling away from and returning to equilibrium."[35] In the danger of the fall and the peace of recovery, Humphrey saw the quest for adventure and the desire for peace. She described the movement between the two actions as the "arc between two deaths."[36] Her emphasis was that one did not "make up" dances, but rather that one *composed* them. This view influenced every serious dance artist who came in contact with her.

Doris Humphrey was considered Martha Graham's equal, and even to this day, some believe Humphrey was the greater artist of modern dance's founding trio because of the methodology she set in place to compose dance. This is an old argument not dissimilar to the equally fierce and forgotten battles between supporters of modern dance or ballet.

Martha Graham performed in one way or another until she died in 1991 at age 97. She had appeared on stage, film, and television. She had taught dancers, written books, given lectures, and graciously accepted awards from everyone from presidents of the United States to university presidents. By sheer force of will she had turned herself into a beauty— a mesmerizing presence both onstage and off.

By contrast, Doris Humphrey was a red-haired, pale-skinned and fragile, fine-boned woman of real beauty and an unassuming nature. By 1944, she had given up performing because of severe arthritis but continued working as an artistic director, choreographer, and teacher for José Limón, the most talented of the Humphrey-Weidman dancers. She died in 1958, revered by students and audiences alike. She was not well known to the world at large and performed too early to be enveloped in the celebrity machine that later caught up with some of the early surviving modern dance pioneers later in the century. Agnes de Mille said of Humphrey, "She cared far less about production, little about recognition, and nothing at all about remuneration. In this, I believe, she was unique, being compelled to create for the joy of the work to the very end of her life."[37]

One of the bylaws of dance—whether ballet or modern— is that movement should respond to music. Boldly, Humphrey composed completely abstract dances to be performed in silence, an idea that is still considered very avant-garde. An early Humphrey solo, 1929's *Life of the Bee*, had her dancing to the sound of someone blowing on a tissue-covered comb mimicking the sound of a bee. In 1931, Humphrey created what is still considered one of her major works: *The Shakers*, a dance for seven people that centered on Humphrey's solo in which "with wide skirts swirling about her, Doris Humphrey lifted her arms, opened her hands, and raised a transfigured face. To the music of a drum, an accordion, and a wordless soprano voice, Humphrey and her dancers re-created a moment in the past for American theater."[38]

Her partner Charles Weidman had simply shown up at Denishawn one day after having seen the company perform in his native Nebraska. He had been an artistically inclined child and was headed toward a career in architecture. "Then," he observed later, "Ruth St. Denis came to the Orpheum Theatre in Lincoln, with her pageant of India, Egypt and Greece, and there was my history of dancing before me. I just put two and two together, and from then on I wanted to do that kind of dancing."[39] Shawn gave him a couple months of instruction and then sent him on the road. Weidman survived his sink-or-swim introduction to performance and went on to create dances himself during the Denishawn years. Shawn capitalized on Weidman's gifts as a mime, creating amusing dances like *Danse Americaine* for the Denishawn repertory. In 1925, Weidman described how this dance was to be performed: "The character is a small mill-town dude. He is the sport of the town and knows it. He is afraid of nothing on earth but the 'skoits'! Remember to keep this spirit of bravado throughout the entire dance. There are no regular fixed steps: it is merely the interpretation of a story by gesture."[40]

Weidman was as involved in creating the technique that came to be associated with the Humphrey-Weidman troupe as Humphrey but balanced out her cerebral and refined approach with his satirical gifts. If Humphrey was drawn to the logical, Weidman was drawn to the illogical. He liked to draw a movement from an everyday incident and then use it in a situation removed from the context in which it had occurred. Much of his work was shaped by his own skill as a brilliant mime and comic and by his talent for finding the telling gesture.

These young experimenters set out not only to create new work, but also to find an audience. They were forced to consider the very problems that had plagued Denishawn: how to support themselves and their dancers while continuing to create and perform. No one wanted to go into Broadway revues again, nor did they want to tour. Teaching classes in their studios helped some but not much. The costs of renting a theater or mounting a production were beyond most of their means. Until they could find a way to financially survive, their artistic endeavors were simply marking time.

In 1929, the Dance Repertory Theater was formed to pool resources and engage a single manager, share advertising costs and even rent a theater for as long as a week. The organizing group consisted of Martha Graham, Doris Humphrey, and Charles Weidman with Helen Tamiris, who had actually suggested this approach. The idea was to find a way to insure both financial support and an audience, thereby addressing the most serious problems facing these dancer-choreographers' futures.

This effort was doomed from the start. None of the big three—Graham, Humphrey and Weidman—considered Tamiris to be an artist on their level. Humphrey and Weidman worried about being "organized to death" as they had been in Denishawn. And Humphrey thought Graham was "a snake."[41] For her part, Graham hated collaboration of any kind, as she was always an intensely single-focused and independent personality. When José Limón stood in the wings watching her dance, she asked the stage manager to tell him she "would not tolerate being watched from the wing."[42]

The Dance Repertory Theater experiment only lasted two seasons. This left Graham, Humphrey, and Weidman right where they had been before: trying to create new dance and get it on stage while somehow supporting themselves financially. Their work, however, had not gone unnoticed.

A young educator named Martha Hill had been "fairly hypnotized" by seeing Graham dance and even briefly became a Graham dancer before turning back to education.[43] Hill became a pioneer in advancing the cause of dance in colleges and universities, beginning first at New York University and then Midwestern colleges. But it would be Bennington College that would become the place where modern dance would find a secure base.

In 1932, Bennington College was founded in southern Vermont with the purpose of establishing an avant-garde education. Martha Hill originated its dance program and received permission to establish summer sessions that would bring in the great modern dance leaders. Not only would they teach, but they would also create their own dances and

Hanya Holm was a German who had come to America in 1931 to start a dance studio intended to teach German Expressionist dance. However, when she found that her American students did not take to the form, she altered the curriculum, and went on to teach at Bennington College with Martha Graham, Doris Humphrey and Charles Weidman in 1934.

perform locally. Nearby, Ted Shawn's New York farm, Jacob's Pillow, opened in 1933 as a summer festival, primarily showcasing his Male Dancers troupe. When both Bennington College and the Jacob's Pillow Festival were up and running, the area became the focus of avant-garde dance. The word spread throughout the nation, although the Bennington group looked down on Shawn's work as reactionary and old-fashioned.

The Bennington program got underway in 1934 with a faculty consisting of Graham, Humphrey, Weidman, and newcomer Hanya Holm. Bringing these maverick experimental dancers into the college curriculum supported the artists in ways beyond their wildest dreams. It was the Depression, yet here they were with free theaters, studios, and production workshops. They had freedom to work, students to teach, theaters to perform in, audiences to see the work—and prestige.

Hanya Holm, the new name among the experimenters, was actually German. She had only come to America in 1931 to set up a dance studio teaching the technique of German Mary Wigman. Germany was the only country other than America to develop modern dance early in the century. Wigman was an important experimenter, influenced by the same movement and emotion theories that had inspired Isadora Duncan. But unlike her contemporary Duncan, Wigman was not afraid of being ugly or performing unattractive subjects. Her work has been associated with the emotional excesses and high drama of German Expressionist art.

When Holm arrived in New York to set up a Mary Wigman school, she found that her American students were not naturally suited to the German Expressionist approach with its distortion and high drama. Wigman gave Holm permission to change her school's American curriculum to make it more suited to American temperament and talents. Had Mary Wigman not been condemned by the Nazis and forced to close all her dance schools, the history of modern dance might have become a joint American and German story. Instead, German Expressionist modern dance as taught by Holm at Bennington and at her studio was folded into the story of the first pioneers of American modern dance, and not as part of a worldwide explosion of new movement. By the time Wigman began to perform and teach once more after World War II, Graham, Humphrey, and Weidman were celebrated artists, and Wigman, major innovator that she was, remained merely an important footnote to the main story.

Modern dance was a fact in the 1940s. No longer a dancer's solitary vision or a choreographer's experiment, modern dance existed as a theater art. Soon the young art form would experience a new generation of rebels, as well as contact with other dance genres.

4

The Reformers and Post-Modern Dance

" . . . dancing is a spiritual exercise in physical form, and . . . what is seen is what it is."

—Merce Cunningham [44]

On the small stage of the Coolidge Theatre at the Library of Congress in Washington, D.C., Martha Graham stood taking a bow. It was October 30, 1944, and at age 50, she had just danced the lead role of a young bride in the premiere of her *Appalachian Spring.* The radiant Graham accepted the applause hand-in-hand with Erick Hawkins, a 35-year-old dancer who had appeared in the stage role of her bride-groom—a role he would play later in real life. Merce Cunningham, a phenomenally talented dancer who had portrayed the frontier preacher, was on her other side. These two men were the first male members of her dance troupe, and within a few years both would have dance companies of

Graham's *Appalachian Spring*, set to an original Aaron Copland score based on Shaker hymns, was the first major commission given to a modern dance-choreographer, and put modern dance on the map as a serious art form.

their own. Composer Aaron Copland's original score, based on a Shaker hymn theme, would go on to win a Pulitzer Prize. It was the first major commission to be given to a modern dance-choreographer and would become the most famous of all Graham's dances. *Appalachian Spring* made it absolutely clear to the world at large that modern dance was no longer to be considered a vaudeville novelty. It had come of age as an art form.

Yet, within a few years of the *Appalachian Spring* premiere, the trio of dancer-choreographers (Martha Graham, Doris

Humphrey, and Charles Weidman) largely responsible for this remarkable theatrical accomplishment would find themselves considered out-of-date. Young dancers, many of them students of the founding threesome, began to look for new subjects to draw upon as they explored ideas of how to move bodies in different ways artistically. The "historic" first modern dance generation wanted to establish itself as uniquely American, taking their subjects from the social and intellectual concerns of their era. Above all, they wanted to be taken seriously and to erase lingering associations of experimental dance with vaudeville and show business.

If modern dance experimenters shared any single view, it was that they were not doing ballet. They wanted to move freely. From their vantage point, the experimenters saw ballet dancers as trapped in an established movement system based on fixed positions of the body, feet and arms, and a performing style that had been codified centuries earlier. Every generation of ballet choreographers and dancers gave ballet a new look, but it was true that they did not change the basic steps and positions. The moderns could not see the way ballet had changed and how it too was in the process of a movement revolution—what the experimenters saw was stagnation. Modern dancers wanted to create new ways of moving suited to their own more democratic time and not with movements they saw as tied to an aristocratic past.

The disdain modern dancers shared for ballet was returned in full measure. Ballet performers and audiences alike thought all the moderns' grand, mythic statements and high-purposed intentions were simply smoke screens covering up the moderns' inability to dance.

Many of the earliest innovators of modern dance were women, but this too was about to change. Dancers from Isadora Duncan to Martha Graham had had the extra burden of proving that a woman could construct a dance that was not about the shape of her legs, but about the content of her mind and spirit. No one had questioned whether or not a woman should dance. This reflected as much as anything the lack of esteem that dance was given as a theater art.

None of this happened immediately. Martha Graham did not retire from performing until 1969 when she was 74 years old. Even then she stayed on stage, usually sitting in a chair and wearing flowing draperies as she introduced her company's performance. Doris Humphrey, however, retired from performing in 1945. She had struggled for years with near crippling arthritis and, finally, as her hip pain became unbearable, was forced to stop performing. Humphrey did not stop working with dance, although her retirement did bring to an end the Humphrey-Weidman Group.

The troupe's most talented dancer, José Limón, went on to found an experimental company of his own in 1946. The Mexican-born Limón, a dancer-choreographer of great presence, took the unique step of asking Doris Humphrey if she would act as an artistic director along with himself. By doing this, Limón insured the continuation of Humphrey's dance theories and actual dance works as he incorporated Humphrey's dances into the repertoire of his newly emerging troupe. The José Limón Dance Company still exists, although its founder died in 1972. It still performs Doris Humphrey's work along with Limón's in an unbroken line that exists nowhere else in modern dance.

Charles Weidman established a studio and a small company of his own at the time Humphrey-Weidman dissolved. He was still living in a room off his rehearsal space and giving Sunday afternoon dance programs when he died in 1975. One of Weidman's most famous students was Bob Fosse, the choreographer who took Weidman's wit and humor and added the sharp edge of jazz dance to became one of America's most important Broadway and Hollywood choreographers, staging such works as *Chicago* and the movie version of *Cabaret*.

While Graham, Humphrey, and Weidman are the recognized pioneers responsible for founding the historic modern dance era, they were not the only modern dancers working in the 1930s and into the 1940s. Among their contemporaries, Helen Tamaris had organized the Dance Repertory Theatre experiment, and Hanya Holm was an important instructor at the Bennington College Dance Festival. Both women created serious dances reflecting the social concerns of their times. Ironically, however, both Tamaris and Holm, as with Fosse, would find their lasting fame choreographing for Broadway.

Tamiris is particularly remembered as one of the first dancer-choreographers to turn to African-American material, and her *Negro Spirituals* is still considered a dance landmark. This was not one dance but a series created through the years 1929 to 1942 using African-American themes and music. The Federal Dance Project, organized in 1935 by the Works Progress Administration as part of the effort to combat the devastating unemployment caused by the Depression, funded Tamiris' *How Long Brethren?* in 1937. It was the first dance to be created by public funding. Yet Tamaris is chiefly remembered today as a Tony award-winning choreographer for the musical *Touch and Go* and even more so for her work with *Annie Get Your Gun.*

Holm remained an important teacher as well as choreographer, and 1937's *Trend*, which she composed while in charge of the workshop group at Bennington College, had the very topical theme of a society being destroyed by false values. In 1941 she established a summer dance institute at Colorado College in Colorado Springs, and she left a legacy of many outstanding students, including Alwin Nikolais, whose work would relight the flame of German Expressionism in American modern dance. Holm, too, found her greatest recognition on Broadway as choreographer for *Kiss Me Kate* (for which she received the New York Drama Critics Award), *My Fair Lady*, and *Camelot.*

Black dance was more than an occasional theme for modern dance, however—it was a thriving dance category of its own. Katherine Dunham and Pearl Primus, two black women who both held doctorates in anthropology, were presenting the genuine article based on field research they had undertaken in Africa and the Caribbean to wildly enthusiastic audiences of every color. Dunham's first important work, *L'Ag'ya*, also supported by the Federal Dance Project, depicted life on Martinique, and she typically presented exciting and glamorous movement and dazzling costumes representing black culture. Primus did this as well, but also focused on grimmer visions of the tribulations of African-American life. These two women anthropologist-performers brought black movement out of the specialty revue or night-club to the concert stage.

In Los Angeles, Lester Horton—a man with wide-ranging interests in dance experimentation and a particular fascination with American Indian culture—formed a dance company in 1932. Horton developed his own technique which centered movement on an unmoving torso with asymmetrical movements of the arms and legs. (Horton's most important student, Alvin Ailey, made this move his own. In dance after dance, Ailey's troupe drew together and leaned their torsos into space, centered and still, while bent-elbowed arms moved in the air like wings suggesting flight, or escape.) Through the years Horton had tried everything from designing outdoor pageants to choreographing nightclub acts and working on movie musicals. He established the first theater in America devoted solely to dance. His most important legacy, however, was that his dance company was the first fully integrated company in America, drawing on African-American, Mexican-American, Japanese, and white dancers. Horton dancers, Alvin Ailey being foremost, carried more than good dancing into the next generation; they brought a colorblind eye to what they did and who did it.

In Martha Graham's company, an extremely talented male dancer, Merce Cunningham, had been singled out repeatedly for praise particularly in his role as the preacher in *Appalachian Spring* and for his fantastic high leaps as March in Graham's ode to Emily Dickinson, *Letter to the World*. While still dancing with Graham, Cunningham began working in creative partnership with experimental composer John Cage, whom he had met in Seattle during his dance student years. When not dancing character roles with Graham, he was experimenting with movement that would be only about dancing. The first solo concert of Cunningham and Cage was given at the Humphrey-Weidman Studio on Sixteenth Street in 1944. *New York Times Herald* critic Edwin Denby said of this performance, "I have never seen a first recital that combined such taste, such technical finish, such originality of dance material," adding that the effect of hearing Cage's "odd timbres" with Cunningham's "dancing has an effect of extreme elegance in isolation."[45]

Born in 1919 and still working to this day, Cunningham has never stopped devising movement that derives its value from what is done in the moment at a particular performance and not from its subject matter, historical, biographical, or psychological meaning. The dance simply exists. That does not mean, however, that he creates simple dances. His interest in both chance and indeterminacy has led to complex dance compositions. He uses chance to decide, often by a flip of a coin or drawing a number, which movement sequence will follow which and who will dance it. The elements thus come together at the performance. It is not the same thing as improvisation because each movement phrase has been set by the choreographer. Since their order is undetermined until the actual performance, they must be able to fit together once the cards are thrown into the air. It is like creating a puzzle where every piece must fit but which is never assembled in the same way.

John Cage (left) with Merce Cunningham. Cunningham was one of the first male members of Graham's dance troupe and collaborated with experimental composer Cage in his own work. Cunningham created dances with little dramatic value, focusing more on the movements themselves.

There is no one point of reference in a Cunningham dance—no central couple, no corps, and no repeating movement patterns to guide the viewer's eye. Even the center of the stage is not necessarily the focus of attention. John Cage's music is created on its own without reference to anything the choreographer is doing, as are the sets and costumes designed by important visual artists. This is as close to total abstraction as anyone has ever come in sustained movement.

The dances Cunningham creates have no inherent dramatic value. They exist as movement and either fascinate or repel by that element alone. In the 1950s at the height of Abstract Expressionism, with Jackson Pollack painting by dribbling color onto a canvas, Cunningham essentially did the same thing by mixing his dance elements by chance at the performance moment. This was—and is—so radical and demanding that audiences routinely walk out of his performances, and even 50 years later, his are regarded as the most avant-garde work.

Cunningham's contemporary, Alwin Nikolais, had been a Bennington dance student who had gone on to become Hanya Holm's assistant before devising his own dance abstractionism. Nikolais experimented with lights, color, and costumes to transform the entire stage space into moving abstractions that engulfed the dancers. He called what he did "dance theater" although none of his dances had a plot. In his high theatricality, he demonstrated his lineage through Holm to German Expressionist dance and its great figure Mary Wigman, who had used masks and wigs to distort her appearance. Nikolais, in fact, had become interested in going into dance when he saw Mary Wigman perform one of her three tours of America in the early 1930s. His choreographic work was like a painting creating itself in front of the audience's eyes. Anonymous dancers stretched inside jersey tubes or between elastic tapes while colors changed and light shifted in size and intensity. Everything on stage—the movements, costumes, and music—all came out of Nikolais' imagination.

Nikolais' 1953 work *Masks, Props, and Mobiles* was not even considered by many critics to be a dance at all, since all the performers wore costumes that disguised or hid their bodies. In one section, they were enclosed in cloth bags which they moved and manipulated from within, creating what looked like modern sculpture pieces. Because Nikolais so often made what were called "dances of sorcery or carnival in which the dancers may be engulfed by an entranced landscape light . . . disappear,

Paul Taylor had worked with Martha Graham and Merce Cunningham before going on to choreograph his own dances. His early avant-garde pieces focused on ordinary movements, such as walking or sitting, but later went on to celebrate dance movement in works such as *Esplanade*.

metamorphose, be imprinted with whirling patterns," critics often did not know quite what to make of what he was doing. Nikolais was not interested in developing dances exploring the human psyche; he wanted to help both dancers and the audience look beyond the personal, saying, "I wanted man to identify with things other than himself." [46]

One other choreographer, Paul Taylor, is an important transitional figure between the historic modern dance pioneers and the free-floating world of modern dance today. Taylor trained at Juillard and the Martha Graham School in New York while assisting painter Robert Rauschenberg and decorating store windows at night. He danced in Merce Cunningham's troupe before moving on to Martha Graham's company in which he was a member for seven years. In his real job, Taylor was partnering Graham herself, who was still dancing in her 60s, in her highly dramatic *Clytemnestra* or dancing in more muscular roles such as that of Hercules in her *Alcestis*. But on his own, Taylor was making a name for himself as someone at the forefront of a very different kind of dance.

He was experimenting with movement that had absolutely nothing to do with Greek myths. He was interested in the way people walked, sat, and ran—in other words, the most ordinary movements of everyday life. So he began exploring movement without using set dance steps. He expanded the idea and asked himself "if dance could be broadened to include everyday moves, so could its accompaniment."

In his studio showcases, he tried out ideas, including *Duet*, in which neither he nor his accompanist moved for the duration of John Cage's *Non Score*. And in *Epic* on the same occasion, Taylor—wearing a business suit and carrying a briefcase—walked back and forth across the stage as the sound of the telephone recorded time announcement played. Abstract visual artist Robert Rauschenberg designed this piece, as he did all of Taylor's 1950 work. Louis Horst, long Graham's musical associate and an important composer in his own right, reviewed Taylor's *Seven New Dances* (which included *Duet* and *Epic*) for *Dance Observer* with four inches of blank space and his initials "L. H." neatly printed at the bottom. Martha Graham shook her finger at Taylor and called him a "naughty boy."[47]

Eventually, Taylor learned to trust his own instinctive

love of movement, going from anti-dance and avant-garde to creating plotless dances of great joyous—and even athletic—movement performed to classical and popular music. As a dancer-choreographer, he did not become frozen in the experiments of one era, although he did occasionally slip some of his earlier experimental ideas into his later work. Twenty years after his *Epic* experiment, Taylor's 1975 work *Esplanade* sent his company walking, running, jumping, sliding, and repeatedly falling to Bach in a glorious burst of lyric dance where ordinary movement became balletic. No one walked out of that performance, and critics filled pages of words describing the beauty of merging this unlikely movement with such sublime classical music.

During the 1960s, America lurched from one internal upheaval to another, beginning with the assassination of President John F. Kennedy. An escalating Vietnam War and universal draft provoked anti-war activities across the country. At the same time, the Civil Rights Movement exploded under the leadership of Dr. Martin Luther King with sit-ins, marches, and campaigns for voting rights. When Dr. King was assassinated in 1968, riots erupted. Yet, unlike the 1930s and '40s when social upheaval inspired the arts and shaped the look of historic modern dance, the sheer violence and personal disaffection of the 1960s seemed to push artists away from these massive problems and further into abstraction.

The new choreographers of the 1960s were inspired by Cunningham, Taylor, and Nikolais, but they went further than these men. They wanted to be as abstract as Cunningham without his complex organization, to push Taylor's experiments with ordinary movement as far as they could go, and to depersonalize their work without using masks or costumes. The Judson Dance Theatre—or Judson Group, as this loose collection of dancers was known—got its name almost 15 years after they had been presenting individual movement experimentation at the Judson Memorial Church on Washington Square in Greenwich Village.

Judson Dance was never a self-conscious movement. People came and went throughout the 1960s, using the studio space at Judson Church, watching each other's work, and taking lessons in dance composition at the Cunningham studio. There were no dues, no rules, and no organization, but there was a manifesto. At one time or another during that decade, it included Trisha Brown, Lucinda Childs, Laura Dean, Simone Forti, Meredith Monk, Robert Rauschenberg, and Twyla Tharp. These dancers were all young, talented, and eager to see if walking, running, or even falling might be dance. Did a dance have to happen on a stage? What if a musician danced? The Judson manifesto, composed by dancer Yvonne Rainer, stated:

NO to spectacle no to virtuosity no to transformations and magic and make-believe no to glamour and transcendency of the star image no to the heroic no to the anti-heroic no to trash imagery no to involvement of performer or spectator no to style no to camp no to seductions of spectator by the wiles of the performer no to eccentricity no to moving or being moved.

These young experimenters were uninterested in historic modern dance with its allusions to myth and psychology. Equally, they dismissed ballet, considering its classical technique to be constraining. They tested the very notion of theatrical dance with pieces like Trisha Brown's *Roof Piece* (1971) in which dancers stationed on rooftops relayed movements which were passed along from roof top to roof top while observers stood on sidewalks far below. David Gordon dropped his trousers and spat during his 1966 solo work *Walks and Digressions* and was roundly booed. Audiences regularly walked out on Judson Church performances, but others took their place. In a continuing series of work, Gordon explored chairs—he sat on them, he fell off them, he tipped them over, and tried just about anything imaginable with a chair. He maddened people, but he challenged and ignited their imaginations as well.

These dancers became the first of the Post-Modern Dance generation. Historic modern dance no longer looked new—its movement solutions were dated. Worse, many of the early experimenters had created techniques full of rules and requirements almost as severe as ballet. Because of what happened at Judson Church, Post-Modern dancers today feel free to move in any way they choose, wear whatever they prefer, move with or without music, and collaborate with anyone—from painters to videographers. The high theatricality of Alwin Nikolais merged into the intense and intellectually demanding experiments of Merce Cunningham, and was then transformed by the ordinary moves Paul Taylor explored into dance of unlimited possibility.

While the Post-Modern movement was underway, another dance revolution was taking place. Alvin Ailey had formed an African-American modern dance troupe in the early 1950s after the death of his mentor Lester Horton. Ailey sought to showcase his own choreography but also to provide creative employment for African-American dancers and choreographers. He wanted to celebrate and reveal the black experience in America. This was not anthropological recreation of traditional black dance or even theatrical versions of them. Instead, this would be modern dance in the purest, historic sense of using movement to portray ideas and social viewpoints on the concert stage.

In 1960, Ailey premiered what would become his company's best-known work, *Revelations*, in which dancers performed to black spirituals. Ailey's masterpiece manages to be both a statement about oppression and yet an explosion of joy. It was the right dance for the right time. As his proud dancers, parasols lifted over their heads, went "Wading in the Water,"

Alvin Ailey was a dancer and choreographer from Lester Horton's racially diverse dance company. Ailey's own work drew on Horton's style of dance based on an unmoving torso and movement expressed through the limbs. Ailey would also provide roles for African Americans in his troupe, and his 1960 work *Revelations* would capture the zeitgeist of the Civil Rights movement.

they took their place in the permanent history of dance. Throughout the 1960s, audiences stood with tears in their eyes, black and white alike, to applaud this pure expression of the hunger of the era to face down and destroy the evils of segregation and bigotry.

The battle to establish modern dance as an American art form was over. Modern dance was acknowledged, and its choreographers became cultural heroes. Martha Graham, for one, received a Presidential Medal of Freedom. Merce Cunningham was awarded a National Medal of Arts and France gave him the Legion d'Honneur. There really was only one last wall to be brought down—that between modern dance and ballet.

5

Fusion

"How do you make a dance? My answer is simple. 'Put yourself in motion.'"

—Twyla Tharp [48]

It was the first time that ballet and modern dance were presented on the same stage. The year was 1959, and ballet's great twentieth century innovator, George Balanchine, artistic director and founding genius of New York City Ballet, reached a hand across the divide between classical ballet and modern dance. He invited Martha Graham to co-choreograph a new two-part work with him called *Episodes*. Using the same music piece, they would each choreograph a dance. The two dances would give the audience a glimpse of how two artists working in different dance traditions used the same music, and how these results would look danced one after the other. It was not a contest or even a challenge, but an opportunity for the

In 1959, renowned ballet choreographer George Balanchine invited Martha Graham to co-choreograph his work *Episodes*, which would set the two influential choreographers' works to the same piece of music. It was a unique moment in time where both modern and ballet shared the stage, and Graham herself performed in her piece, despite being 65 years old and suffering from arthritis.

choreographers, their dancers, and the audience to see just how profoundly different, or alike, the work would be. It was a symbolic white flag, a moment of respect, in the ongoing war between the modern and classical camps.

Balanchine picked the music of Anton Von Webern, a composer whose music was experimental and atonal. The composer used a broken melody line, odd combinations of instruments, and made extremely brief compositions. A Webern symphony movement was often less than two minutes long. Balanchine's particular genius was for choreographing the internal structure of music. He liked turning the mathematics of modern music into figures on stage. Graham also used modern music, but the composers she worked with most successfully, like Aaron Copland in *Appalachian Spring*, gave her enough melody line to use music as a way to shape characters and establish mood. She was not interested in making dances that looked like an abstract geometry equation. She wanted emotion and high drama. Having risen to the challenge of performing back-to-back and face-to-face with New York City Ballet at City Center, Graham accepted Balanchine's music choice.

At 65 years of age, Graham was theoretically long past her dancing days. However, she could not give it up. Nothing in Graham's life mattered more to her than performing. Famously she had said, "The center of the stage is where I am."[49] Her highly dramatic approach to movement, with spectacular twisting falls to the ground and deep body contractions expressing yearning, were synonymous in most people's minds with modern dance. Balanchine's great contribution to classical ballet was to transform it into a sleek, abstract movement form we now call neo-classic ballet. He sometimes used stories, sets, and costumes, but only occasionally. The pure Balanchine style, with its high leg extensions, intricate footwork and speed performed by dancers wearing black practice leotards, was as foreign to nineteenth century classical ballet in its way as was the Graham style.

Graham decided to base her dance on the historic standoff between Queen Elizabeth of England and her cousin Mary, Queen of Scots. Although she was well past her dancing prime,

Graham herself danced the role of Mary. She selected New York City Ballet dancer Sallie Wilson to perform the part of Queen Elizabeth and two other ballet men to hold up banners. Similarly, Balanchine asked that Paul Taylor, then dancing in the Graham company to great acclaim, perform a variation in his section. This was the extent of actual performance interaction between the modern camp and the ballet citadel.

The opening performance, on May 14, 1959, was a personal triumph for Graham. The audience spontaneously rose as soon as she appeared onstage. No one who saw Graham dance in her last years forgot the sheer force of personality that hit the audience. She dominated stage space, obscuring both her age and limited physical abilities. Sixty-five years old or not, Graham's Mary was a commanding presence, and, at least in this danced version, Wilson's Elizabeth—a slight, much younger woman—was at a severe disadvantage. Although Graham's feet were crippled with arthritis and she could barely stand or walk, she danced magnificently. George Balanchine wisely stayed backstage and let Martha take the bows.

The critics weighed in with reviews that tended to favor whichever of the two geniuses they most admired. Those who disliked Balanchine saw his section as "inhuman" and "perverse." Graham's critics saw her section as "melodramatic" and "the same old steps."[50] *Episodes* was just that—an episode—and not the beginning of any true relationship between the two figures who as much as any were making the United States the world capital of dance.

Within a short time, *Episodes* would appear a quaint event. The 1960s were unfolding and Balanchine was headed into his years of acknowledged greatness where his work would come to dominate ballet. More importantly for modern dance, though, the Judson dancers were beginning the experiments that would lead to yet another refocusing of modern dance.

The emerging Post-Modern dancers superficially would appear the least likely candidates to bridge the world between modern and ballet. What could be less balletic than dancing in sneakers or climbing a fire escape and calling it a dance?

Yet once again modern dance was about to be jolted by someone trained from within. A Judson Dance Theater experimenter, a young woman from California named Twyla Tharp, would open up the first real artistic interchange between modern dance and ballet.

When Twyla Tharp arrived in New York City in 1961 as a mid-year transfer student at Barnard College, her major was art history, but her real interest was dance. As a child, she had studied ballet, tap, violin, and baton twirling with a self-imposed schedule of school, lessons, and practice that began at 6 A.M. with "Put practice clothes on" and ended 15 hours later at 9:30 P.M. with "Eat supper, get ready for bed." [51] As a young adult in New York City, Tharp's willpower remained as ferocious as ever. In addition to college, she combined lessons in ballet and every form of modern dance offering classes with her college studies. She fell in love with Balanchine's work and would have studied at his School of American Ballet, but as she says, "Fortunately his school was closed to the general public; had I been allowed access to Balanchine, I probably would have signed up for life and never developed my own idiom." [52]

Her classes ranged from ballet to Martha Graham and Merce Cunningham and even the Broadway Jazz style of Bob Fosse. Tharp was accumulating an "encyclopedic" knowledge of different dance techniques and the possibility of making out of "this swirling kaleidoscope of choices . . . a kind of a dance no one else could do." [53] Still an undergraduate at Barnard, Tharp focused on Paul Taylor and simply kept hanging around in his studio until he half-jokingly put her in his company. Taylor described her as "a little person with enormous magnetism and push—a brash but lovable

Twyla Tharp joined Paul Taylor's company by hanging around constantly until he took her in. Her own experimental dances employed many different dance styles, reflecting her own wide-ranging knowledge, and set her dances to music such as jazz or the songs of the Beach Boys.

Munchkin."[54] She finished her Barnard degree but skipped graduation in order to go on tour with Taylor's company.

It was not long before Tharp began working on her own experimental dances, working in the Judson Church gym. Her first dances were presented at Judson as well, but while her work looked Judson, philosophically it was different. Her

1966 *Re-Moves* was a four-section work done in silence and involved the dancers moving around a large plywood box. In the final section, the dancers sat inside the box. After a long period of silence, they emerged but not to take a bow. Tharp had declared an audience was superfluous, a practice she continued for five years "because I was worried, first, that there would be no audience, and second, that even if there was one, they would hate what we did."[55] Tharp herself saw *Re-Moves* as representing the bleakness of the Vietnam era in which it was constructed. Even in works as challenging as this, Tharp was polishing up an inclusive dance style which called for "trigger-quick shifts of weight from toe-to-heel, rapid changes of direction."[56] Her choreography compacted "innumerable slivers of movement." She resisted the Judson Manifesto, saying that all the Judson no's (to spectacle, virtuosity, transformations, magic, and make-believe) "would become my yeses."[57]

In 1973, experimenter Tharp virtually shouted "Yes" when she accepted a commission from Robert Joffrey to create a new work for his Joffrey Ballet Company. This would be no *Episodes* with ballet and modern greats performing cautiously and separately on the same stage space. This was Robert Joffrey, an innovative ballet director whose small troupe survived on an eclectic repertoire of twentieth century ballets and newly commissioned work, working with Twyla Tharp, a very flexible, imaginative choreographer who had made her name as an experimenter but was well grounded in ballet. Tharp would use some of her own company members, but they were making it happen for the Joffrey Ballet.

The resulting dance, *Deuce Coupe*, was set to the Beach Boys' pop songs that Tharp had grown up with in California. The backdrop was long paper rolls of original graffiti art. While the main body of the dance spilled across the stage with both Tharp and Joffrey dancers doing Tharp quick changes between bugaloo, jazz, ballet, and modern steps, a solitary ballerina moved across the stage, methodically assuming all the positions of ballet. In a very interesting moment in dance and theater history, ballet visually intersected the modern dance realm. Tharp herself noted: "In 1959, Balanchine and Graham had shared a program . . . but my collaboration with the Joffrey marked the first time ever that a modern company performed in a ballet."[58] It was a critical and box-office knockout.

Deuce Coupe was such a phenomenal success that Robert Joffrey quickly signed up Tharp to create another dance for his company, and eight months later in 1974, she presented *As Time Goes By,* danced to Haydn. Working with the Joffrey had its drawbacks, though. The troupe survived by touring, and novelty is what brought audiences to see it. The Tharp pieces were huge novelties to audiences unused to ballet companies dancing to popular music or performing modern dance steps. Tharp thought she had made "well crafted dance(s), challenging and developing techniques and traditions . . ." but found the audiences were responding to bright lights, loud music and "sexy people."[59]

The Joffrey successes were not ignored by the larger, more established ballet companies. The American Ballet Theatre (ABT) had recently hired Russian dancer Mikhail Baryshnikov, who had defected from the Soviet Union the summer of 1974. Baryshnikov was the latest in a series of spectacular ballet dancers who had fled from the Soviet's superb but highly institutionalized and confining ballet tradition. Rudolf Nureyev's defection to the West in 1961 had been the first, and he had electrified the ballet world and inspired a stream of other Soviet trained dancers to flee as well.

These dancers were not only magnificent talents, but they also became cultural heroes in the Cold War-era standoff between the democracies of the West and the totalitarian Communist system of the East. They drew people to dance not simply to see their extraordinary talents, but also to applaud their personal courage as well. When American Ballet Theatre approached Tharp about making a dance for Baryshnikov, she was initially hesitant. Here was a dancer being called one of the greatest, perhaps *the* greatest, to ever perform. Alvin Ailey said to her, "Are you going to do a ballet for Baryshnikov? You've got to be nuts. You'll be eaten alive."[60]

Baryshnikov, however, had not defected so that he could perform exactly the same dances as those in the Russian repertory. He was in love with American culture, modern dance, and experimentation of all kind. The dancer he personally most admired was Fred Astaire. It was Baryshnikov himself who had suggested the Tharp commission after seeing what she had done for Joffrey Ballet. He settled the question once and for all when Tharp came to watch him during an ABT rehearsal. He suddenly interrupted what he was doing to turn a cartwheel and do a somersault, landing literally at Tharp's feet. "Take me," he said. "I promise I'll never be boring or predictable."[61] One of the most intriguing partnerships in dance was born in that instant.

The dance Tharp made for Baryshnikov, *Push Came to Shove*, was a mingling of everything imaginable—not just ballet and modern, but also jazz and ragtime and pure Tharp nonsense. She picked the name because it suggested the "juxtapositions in the ballet: the old classical forms of ballet versus jazz and its own classicism, the East of Misha, the West of Me . . . then too I knew it would please Misha: the name of the great Kirov instructor, responsible for Misha's development . . . was Alexandr Pushkin."[62]

The dance premiered on January 9, 1976. Dancing to ragtime and Haydn, one of the acknowledged greatest male dancers of all time was transformed into a "bowler-hatted, womanizing rogue." It was an astonishing success and established a partnership between Baryshnikov and Tharp that would be both personal and professional. Push really had come to shove in the dance world.

A precursor to Tharp's style of pop blending was American choreographer Jerome Robbins' 1944 ballet *Fancy Free*, which combined ballet with jazz music.

Essentially Twyla Tharp threw all the cards up in the air, catching and using those that suited her. She was not the first choreographer to shuffle steps from different dance techniques into one dance. Modern dancers as early as Ruth St. Denis had been familiar with ballet technique and freely used ballet poses or turns where they worked. Ballet dancers often danced in less formal classical works. Jerome Robbins' 1944 *Fancy Free*, a breezy, jazzy ballet of three sailors on leave in New York City, is only one of many examples.

What Tharp did differently was to blend steps together, stringing jazz, ballet, tap, and modern in one movement phrase. There was no signal she was changing from modern to ballet. A rolling modern Tharp torso shifted up into an airborne ballet *jeté* and landed with the turned-in bent knees of jazz. She was not a modern dancer who worked in ballet—she was a dancer who threaded together steps from tap, ballet, modern, jazz, and ballroom seamlessly.

Push Comes to Shove was a defining moment in dance, and its effects are felt even now almost 30 years later. By the late 1970s, the sharp divide between modern dance and ballet began to disappear. This did not mean that everyone was happy, however. Modern dance purists scolded Tharp for abandoning her earlier important experiments to work in "mainstream" ballet and theater. Ballet commentators worried that ballet was not producing enough of its own new choreographers and relying too much on the moderns. Endless discussions have been held as to whether modern dancers or classical ballet dancers are better trained.

This late 1970s experimentation was the beginning of what has come to be called the Dance Boom or Dance Explosion. Whether the audience started to come to dance performances to see a "novelty" dance or a famous Russian or even out of simple curiosity turned out not to matter. An audience for dance was developing, one which was able to enjoy it as theater art whether it understood the fine points of dance technique or knew all the details of a choreographer's philosophy. Audiences found that watching David Parsons appear to fly through the air as he danced in flickering strobe lights was thrilling enough, so that it did not matter whether they knew Parsons had danced with Paul Taylor's troupe and represented a line of modern dance tracing right back to Martha Graham.

The National Endowment for the Arts established a dance touring program that sent smaller modern companies touring across America to perform in theaters and at universities. This was not vaudeville or a sequestered college summer session. Even when the Dance Touring program was cut back in the 1980s, companies continued to tour, having established audiences for their work across the country. American modern dance spread overseas where important companies, including the Netherlands Dance Theater in The Hague and the Frankfurt Ballet in Germany, have flourished with American dancers as artistic directors and choreographers.

Meanwhile, colleges and universities across the country included dance programs in their curriculum. Dance companies sprang up in the wake of the coursework and with the chance to see the professionals on tour. Students at Dartmouth College put together a funny, athletic, and professional troupe called Pilobolus, which specialized in contorting themselves into odd body sculptures onstage. Four more dance companies can claim descent from Pilobolus: Momix, Crowsnest, ISO, and BodyVox. If it is possible to see the Nikolais multimedia dance theater tradition in their work, it is not necessary or even intended.

In 1985—almost 25 years after David Gordon was making bizarre dances falling off chairs at Judson Church—Baryshnikov, then the American Ballet Theatre's artistic director, commissioned Gordon to do a work for the big ballet company. In Gordon's dance *Field, Chair and Mountain,* the ballet dancers carried around folding chairs which they opened and then arranged in ballet corps patterns. The dancers clambered upon the chairs and danced upon them.

Totally abstract and experimental dance choreography continues as well. Judson dancer Steve Paxton experimented with a system of *contact improvisation,* where partners reacted to each other as the other moved. Contact Improv started in dance studios and has entered into dance curriculum and is even performed as concert dance. It is almost like a game. Because the dancers slide and fall, needing to be caught or braced by the partner, it is more like an art sport. The tension for the dancers, and for anyone watching, resides in the trust the dancers must have in each other and how quickly they must respond. The partners constantly touch as "the inevitable result of leaning, sliding, twisting to follow the current of movement and play with the tug of gravity."[63]

Modern dance's integration with other styles and genres is evident in Mark Morris' *The Argument*, shown here with Morris performing with classical cellist Yo-Yo Ma. Morris' sense of whimsy is evident in his own take on *The Nutcracker*, entitled *The Hard Nut*, which was choreographed in 1991 and continues to be an annual event in New York City.

Probably no dancer-choreographer gives a better picture of where modern dance is in the early twenty-first century than Mark Morris. Born in 1956, his life mirrors the Dance Explosion. In the 1960s, while the Judson dancers were beginning their experiments, Morris was just a little boy in Seattle, Washington.

This child loved to dance, and when he saw José Greco's Spanish dance troupe, he insisted upon taking flamenco lessons. By the time he was 14 years old, Morris himself was teaching Spanish dance. In order to keep this hyper-talented, hyper-curious young man busy, his flamenco teacher directed him to ballet. He absorbed movement like a sponge. Then he became infatuated with Balkan folk dances and music, and as a teenager added a stint with the Koleda Folk Ensemble, a semi-professional Balkan folk company.

Because Morris was growing up in the era of the Dance Touring program, living in Seattle did not prevent him from becoming familiar with companies like Paul Taylor's, whose company visited regularly, or Martha Graham's. The Joffrey Ballet spent long weeks every summer resident in the Seattle area and he haunted their performances, especially loving the funky *Deuce Coupe* by Tharp.

When Morris began dancing professionally, he had trained and was interested in performing everything. That is exactly what he did—he performed in a ballet troupe (Eliot Feld), a modern dance company (Lar Lubovitch), and a Post-Modern ensemble (Laura Dean). He even worked with the outsized talent who started this whole wide-open dance scene, Twyla Tharp, when she choreographed the film *Hair* in 1979. In other words, Morris was the living exemplar of the almost unlimited possibilities of Post-Modern dance. When his own company had its first performance in 1980, it was held in Merce Cunningham's studio.

Gregarious, funny, and phenomenally talented, Morris fit in anywhere. He was not a modern dancer who wanted to dance in silence or pick his music by chance. Since he openly relished everything from Rumanian folk songs to Schubert, he quickly became noted as a choreographer who also was a music connoisseur. As a performer, he physically managed to be a uniquely Post-Modern dancer as well. He is large—in fact, he is a huge, barrel-chested man, making him a very unlikely candidate for a dancer. When Morris comes onstage, it is like seeing a preposterous hippo in dance shoes. Then he moves and is as elegant in his own way as Baryshnikov. His company is full of dancers of varying sizes and ages. He also is openly gay in a very flamboyant way, which is a part of his stage persona. Morris plays with spoofs on cross-dressing, even costuming some of his male dancers in fluffy ballerina tutus but always in the context of the dance.

In 1991 Morris choreographed *The Hard Nut*, which is his version of ballet's Christmas classic *The Nutcracker*. It was created and first presented at the Theatre Royal de la Monnaie in Brussels, Belgium when Morris was its dance artistic director. The generous resources of Belgium's national opera house were put at his disposal to create a sumptuous anti-*Nutcracker*. Morris set the Christmas party not in a lovely nineteenth century European mansion but in an ordinary 1960s American living room with white vinyl couches and a white plastic Christmas tree. The partygoers wear bell-bottomed pants and hot-colored minidresses. When the mysterious family friend Drosselmeier arrives, he does not present the heroine with toy soldiers and a dancing doll to entertain her. Instead he brings robots and a life-sized Barbie. The traditional mock battle between the mice and the toy soldiers becomes a contest between big, hairy rats which fight G.I. Joes. In the "Waltz of the Snowflakes," both men and women—wearing fluffy white tutus and hats that look like the swirled tops of Dairy Queen ice cream cones—dance, and they all toss snowflakes merrily in the air. Morris himself danced the Arabian variation at the opening, wearing slinky veils, ankle bells, and sunglasses.

The Hard Nut is outrageous, funny, and extravagantly inventive. It now plays annually in New York as an alternative to the better known traditional versions. This is how modern dance works—it is always personal art. It is a history of individual artists, each an intriguing personality. Some have the high drama of Martha Graham. Others seek the high plateau of

Merce Cunningham's cerebral experimentation. Still others want to soar across stage like Paul Taylor or see how it would work to add in hip-hop or Balinese moves.

There will be more of these original dancers in the twenty-first century—stubborn yet talented people who will insist on working in their own odd ways. There undoubtedly will be a manifesto issued now and then. In its exuberance, ingenuity and innovation, modern dance reflects the American spirit. Like jazz, hip-hop, and bluegrass, it was born here. Modern dance's story is one of expanding inclusion and equality, and it shows no sign of going away.

A Modern
Dance Class

"Girl or boy, gifted or clumsy, learn then, if you can, to dance. You will stand up straighter and walk prouder the rest of your life. And you will be kinder and more polite in all physical matters, and less afraid."

—Agnes de Mille [64]

There is nothing neat and tidy about studying modern dance. Unlike ballet—where one enters a beginning class and is instructed in the basic positions of the body, arms, legs and feet in order to develop the movement vocabulary that a student ballet dancer will build on indefinitely—there is no standard introduction to modern dance. No fixed modern dance terminology exists either, and confusingly enough, all modern dance techniques use ballet terms, tap terms, and even jazz dance terms to describe movements which may or may not be identical to the actual ballet, tap, or jazz dance

Noted choreographer Bob Fosse shown directing dancers in a studio. Some modern dance classes are taught in the particular techniques of famous choreographers such as Martha Graham or Merce Cunningham, whose movement systems could be taught.

moves. This does not mean that there is no actual discipline of modern dance. Rather, it means that every modern dancer gets to experience something of the great exhilaration of the pioneer modern dancers as each finds his or her own way to dance.

Hundreds of modern dance styles are taught across the United States. Some focus on the technique of one major modern dance figure. Most serious modern dancers have taken classes at one time or another in the techniques of Martha Graham, Limón-Humphrey, Lester Horton, Merce Cunningham, and Mary Wigman. These particular techniques are studied in part not only because the people were great dancers, but because they made movement systems that could be taught. Some of these are almost as formal and codified as ballet. Then there are brilliant instructors who have been influenced by Paul Taylor or Twyla Tharp or some other currently working modern choreographer who offer slightly different and still emerging approaches to modern dance. Any of these and countless other techniques can offer fine introductions to modern dance.

To make matters even more complicated, the beginning modern dancer usually can find the option of taking a general introductory course on modern movement, often called Creative Dance or Expressive Movement. The quality of these courses ranges widely, but they usually emphasize work that centers the body through breathing and learning to move freely and comfortably on bare feet. A general Creative Dance class is often not very different from the kinds of freestyle self-exploratory movement that Isadora Duncan and the early twentieth century adherents of eurhythmics advocated.

In one way, a modern dance class will be exactly like a ballet, tap, or jazz class. It will have a certain etiquette that is required of all students. The student will wear appropriate clothing for the class, and this includes footwear if any. In most cases, the costume will be a leotard which enables the student to move freely and the instructor to easily see whether the student's movements are correct. Being prompt to every class is important. Every class will begin with some warm-up movements and then proceed to the increasingly more difficult and strenuous exercises. It is not possible to come in late and catch up, which is also rude to the instructor and the other students.

The dance teacher instructs by demonstrating and explaining the movement, and then the class will repeat this movement. Look for a class where the instructor is actively engaged in the student's work, and is walking around, doing corrections both by talking and by actually physically moving a student's foot or shoulder into the correct place. There really is only one way to learn dance, and that is from another dancer, so corrections are essential. In most cases, the class takes place in a studio with a wall of mirrors. This allows the student as well as the instructor to focus on details of the movement. Good dancers are able to assess their own movements and make adjustments and corrections as they watch themselves. The studio will have a long *barre* along the wall for balance while performing exercises on one side of the body. The barre is used primarily for ballet exercises and rarely with modern steps.

Class will be held to taped music, but it is not unusual for a modern dance class to be accompanied by someone on piano and often with drums. Live accompaniment allows the instructor to stop and start the exercise as well as to change the tempo as they go along. Modern dance classes have been held to the sound of people reading poetry. When the class is finished, it is appropriate to give the instructor a round of applause before leaving the floor. This dance tradition comes from ballet where class traditionally ends with a *reverence*, or bow, on the part of the students, followed by the students applauding the instructor. The structure of the dance lesson is a reminder to the student that the work is serious, and that those who wish to run, play, laugh, interrupt, and do whatever they want may do so only on their own time. A professional dancer is one of the most disciplined people in the world.

How does one select a modern dance class? The simplest answer to the question is to visit the modern dance classes offered in the student's area. Classes are available in private studio classes, and in professional high schools for those in large metropolitan areas. There are many university and college dance departments, and these may have opportunities including public performances and seminars. If the student is near a city where touring companies perform, there will be opportunities to take master classes with the professionals just as Mark Morris did. In fact, if Morris' company is on tour, it would be possible to take classes with his company.

Sitting in on classes gives a prospective student an opportunity to get the feel for different techniques and to gauge their own reactions. Starting in one technique does not mean it is impossible to learn others in the future. Not every beginner feels ready to tackle a Martha Graham contraction. Since virtually every modern dance instructor is different and usually a disciple of one particular technique, it is a good idea to visit before enrolling. The major techniques a prospective student is likely to find available include:

Martha Graham classes have four parts and are done on the center of the floor. They begin with floorwork, which involves actually lying, as well as sitting, on the ground to do exercises intended to stretch and strengthen the torso. These include breathing exercises of inhaling and exhaling coordinated with contractions of the pelvic muscles which are Graham's central movement device. There is nothing pedestrian about Graham movements; even the floor exercises are dramatic. The class proceeds to exercises standing in one place, which include *pliés* (bends) and *battement* (beats of the feet and legs). The ballet terminology is used, but the Graham dancer does not seek ballet's extreme turnout of the hip and feet. The class moves on to work with elevation (leaping), and finally with falling to the ground.

Graham technique is full of falls, and she herself was famous for a swirling spiral fall to the ground as treacherous to perform as it looked. Paul Taylor, Merce Cunningham, and Alwin Nikolais are only a handful of the important students of Graham technique.

Merce Cunningham classes begin in the center of the floor as well, but standing. Here the class does back stretches and pliés. There will be work on back curves, tilts, and twists. Attention will be given to exercises that increase feet articulation (the ability to use any part of your foot) and speed of footwork. Normally a Cunningham class does not do floorwork, and it often looks like a ballet class, though the students are standing in the studio instead of working at an attached ballet barre. The movements have no inherent drama like Graham's but may be speeded up or slowed down over and over to train the dancer to have the quickest possible response to movement. Cunningham's studio launched the Post-Modern Judson movement. His technique shares the honors with Graham for being most influential and is as abstract as Graham is dramatic.

Lester Horton movement is very well known even if his name may sound less familiar than Graham's or Cunningham's. Through his famous students (Alvin Ailey especially), the flat back projected forward into space with arms extending laterally are movement images everyone recognizes. Horton classes usually stay in the center of the floor as well, and only occasionally on the floor with attention given to strengthening the torso. It is a very exhilarating as well as demanding way to move, and even the classes can look like a performance.

Limón-Humphrey is the distillation of Doris Humphrey's fall and recovery movement theories. There are many important students of Limón-Humphrey-Weidman who, like the Horton students, have kept this more lyric modern dance methodology alive. Doris Humphrey's philosophy remains at

The Limón-Humphrey technique, named after José Limón (left) and Doris Humphrey, teaches Humphrey's fall and recovery movement theories. Her philosophy stressed that emotion should come before movement.

the core of the technique, stressing that emotion comes before movement. In addition to Humphrey's most famous student José Limón, Sybil Shearer and Anna Halprin have passed this way of moving into succeeding generations.

A serious modern dance student usually studies ballet and tap. Sometimes it is helpful to do this before beginning modern dance classes. All of the great modern dancers know the basic ballet steps and positions. The reason for this is simple: ballet gives a useful terminology for all dancers. Even if modern dancers never attempt to have a fully turned-out leg, they will take classes and study choreography where they are asked to do something in a turned out position. For a modern dancer, this means a comfortable turnout and not the extreme ballet position, which is only achieved even by ballet dancers after years of rigorous practice.

All modern dance instructors scatter ballet terminology in their classes. Routinely, they ask a class to put their feet in second position, or even do a *tendu*. Just as routinely, they mix ballet with simple commands to move up or go down. Sometimes the instructor will ask for a battement and just as casually ask the dancers to lift their legs to the side, which is the same thing as a battement. In other words, ballet is dance's universal language, and it helps in any dance form one might study.

Tap is very useful for a modern dancer as well. Learning to create beats with the feet teaches the dancer about rhythm with his or her own body. Since the dancers are creating the beat and the sound, they experience sound and rhythm as a total body experience. This is different from dancing to music or even to drumming. If a modern dancer has any interest at all in going into jazz dance, he or she will find that the tap terms are jazz's basic terminology. A ball and chain is a tap sound that moves from the ball of one foot to the ball of another. It can be Twyla Tharp instructing: right ball change, *sur le cou-de-pied* on the left. Translated from tap and ballet, that means: shift your weight from the ball of the left foot to the right, and then place your right foot on the ankle of your left leg.

There are two magazines about dance that will help any modern dance student. *Dance Magazine* is aimed at dance

Tap dance, which involves special shoes that create loud percussive sounds, can be useful for the modern dance student, especially in teaching rhythm. Those who are interested in jazz dance will also find tap to be important as well.

professionals and the general dance audience, and *Dance Spirit* is aimed at the student and young dance professional, as well as anyone interested in a dancer's world. Both magazines regularly list schools, summer sessions, camps, and other training opportunities. They have college issues and special sections on performing arts high schools, as well as listings for the professional giving auditions and job listings. If there are no modern dance classes where the would-be student lives, the student can search these periodicals and write to information offices of modern dance camps or short-term programs nearby to inquire about eligibility. Much of this, including checking the magazines, can be done online.

Modern dance is still about finding a personal way of moving, whether in the classroom or on the stage. There is someone right now experimenting with new ideas for a dance. Maybe they are doing it in front of the mirror in their bedroom or twirling around and watching their reflection in the glass of a sliding door. They are thinking about movement. Sometimes they jump off a bus and add an extra hop just for the pleasure of doing it. They are movers. Fifty years from now, or even sooner, some of these preoccupied, dedicated, hardworking future dancer-choreographers will be added to yet another history of modern dance. Everyone will still complain that "modern dance" is an old-fashioned term, but they will keep using it anyway.

Glossary

ballet. From the Italian *ballare*. As theatrical dance, it is an art form based on a specific technique involving a fixed set of steps and positions developed over hundreds of years. Non-specifically, the term is used by all choreographers to describe a concert dance. For example, it would not be incorrect to call Alvin Ailey's dance *Revelations* a ballet, although it actually is modern dance.

barre. A horizontal wooden handrail used by dancers to maintain balance while doing studio exercises. It is used by both modern and ballet dancers, but principally in classical ballet classes. A ballet dancer places one hand lightly on the barre while doing exercises that require balance.

battement. A beating movement of an extended leg or foot. This is a ballet term but is widely used in all forms of dance.

choreography. From Greek, literally meaning "dance-writing." It is the steps and patterns of a particular dance. The person who designs the steps and patterns is called the choreographer.

contact improvisation. A playful improvisation between two or more dancers in which they respond to each other's movement as it occurs in the moment. Thus, dancers must react very quickly to protect themselves from falling or slipping if not instantaneously supported. Often called an art sport. Steve Paxton, a Judson Theater experimenter, is credited with creating the movement form.

contraction-release. The fundamental movement of the Martha Graham technique. It refers to movement in the torso as the dancer inhales (contracts) and complete exhalation (release).

cou-de-pied. A ballet position that puts the working foot on the ankle of the supporting leg. The term is used in other dance forms as well.

Dalcroze. Emile Jaques-Dalcroze (1865–1950) was a student of Francois Delsarte. He furthered the Desarte method by designing a system of training music students to understand rhythm by translating sounds into physical movements. It could be, and was, applied to dance as well and influenced many early modern dancers. He called the system "rhythmic gymnastics" and it became known as *eurythmics*.

Delsarte. Francois Delsarte was a French music teacher in the early nineteenth century who developed a system known as the Delsarte Method in which performers were taught to develop the expressive-ness of their bodies. He ranged his movements into three categories (eccentric, concentric, and normal) and three zones (head, torso, and limbs.) It was a very influential methodology for all the early modern dance pioneers, as well as several generations of gymnasts and students of calisthenics.

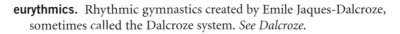

eurythmics. Rhythmic gymnastics created by Emile Jaques-Dalcroze, sometimes called the Dalcroze system. *See Dalcroze.*

German Expressionism. In the early twentieth century, Expressionism dominated the arts in Germany and Central Europe. The artist stressed the emotional content of experience and symbolic meaning in objects. In dance, these ideas were explored by Mary Wigman (1886–1973) who taught and performed a technique emphasizing dramatic intensity and distortion of body shapes. Wigman was one of the most important pioneers of modern dance, but her career and influence were interrupted when she was condemned by the Nazis and forced to shut down her schools. She did not resume teaching and performing until 1949.

leotard. A tight garment covering the torso usually worn over tights which cover the legs. It is the basic practice costume for any dance study. There actually was a man named Jules Leotard, a French gymnast who is credited with creating with the costume.

modern dance. An unsatisfactory term usually used to describe any experimental concert dance that is not classical ballet or ethnic/folk dance. It was considered an old-fashioned term by the 1940s, when even Martha Graham called her company Martha Graham Contemporary Dance. The term still continues largely out of common usage.

plié. A bend of the knee, often in preparation for jumps or turns. A ballet term, widely used in all forms of dance.

Post-Modern. A catch-all phrase covering experimental dance from Merce Cunningham to the present. Essentially, it separates the post-Cunningham experimenters from the so-called Historic Modern Dancers. Generally, it favors abstraction of content, the cerebral over the highly emotional, and movement representing many techniques. It can, however, include any and all of the above as well.

tendu. A ballet term for any move that is stretched or held. Used widely in other dance forms.

turnout. The outward rotation of the legs from the hips at a 90-degree angle. This turnout enables a dancer to move quickly on either side of the body as well as forward and backward without breaking the line of the leg. A ballet position widely used in all forms of dance.

tutu. The ballerina's costume consisting of a fitted bodice and a bouffant skirt made of many layers of net or tulle. It is derived from French slang for the bottom.

95

1900 American experimental dancer Loie Fuller dances in her own pavillon at the Paris Exposition; American experimenters Isadora Duncan and Ruth St. Denis are in the audience.

1914 Ruth St. Denis selects Ted Shawn as dance partner; the two dancers subsequently marry in August of that year.

1915 Denishawn, the first important school teaching new dance methods, opens in Los Angeles with name created out of the names of founders Ruth St. Denis and Ted Shawn. Name Denishawn used for their dance troupe as well.

1920 Isadora Duncan establishes Dance Institute in Soviet Union after period of fame in France.

1925–26 Denishawn tours the Orient, Japan, China, Burma, India (Pakistan), Ceylon (Sri Lanka), Malaya (Malaysia), Java, and the Philippines.

1926 Martha Graham, former Denishawn dancer, has her first independent solo dance concert.

1927 Isadora Duncan dies.

1928 Doris Humphrey and Charles Weidman, former Denishawn dancers, form their own troupe composed of other former Denishawn dancers and hold the first dance concert by a modern dance ensemble.

1929 Martha Graham premieres *The Heretic,* her first concert dance for a group of dancers.

1934 The Bennington College School of Dance summer program, the first important college program in modern dance, begins with instructors Martha Graham, Ruth Humphrey, Charles Weidman, and many others on the faculty.

1934 Lester Horton establishes a dance company in Los Angeles, which becomes the first fully racially integrated dance company in America.

1944 Merce Cunningham, a member of Martha Graham troupe, performs his first solo dance concert with John Cage providing musical accompaniment.

1948 Lester Horton establishes the first theater in America dedicated solely to presenting dance.

1953 Merce Cunningham establishes his own dance company with John Cage as musical director.

1957 Paul Taylor, a member of Martha Graham troupe, presents *Seven New Dances,* which includes not moving to "non-music."

1958 Alvin Ailey, a Lester Horton dancer, establishes the Alvin Ailey American Dance Theater, continuing Horton's emphasis on inclusion, particularly in creating opportunities for African-American dancers and choreographers.

1960s Beginning of Judson Dance Theater, a free-flowing and changing group of avante-garde dance experimenters working at a Greenwich Village church, reject traditional technique and explore "ordinary" movement as dance.

1961 Paul Taylor establishes his own modern dance troupe.

1965 Twyla Tharp, at one time a Judson Theater experimenter, leaves the Paul Taylor Company to form her own modern dance company.

1976 Twyla Tharp choreographs *Push Comes to Shove* for Mikhail Baryshnikov at American Ballet Theater in a successful blend of modern, ragtime, and ballet, signaling an explosion in dance and blending of dance technique of all types from modern to ballet.

1980s–present
Post-Modern Dance Explosion. Creative fusion of dance techniques leads to wide acceptance of experimental dance.

The following videos are all available through Princeton Book Company, which specializes in dance books and videos (800-220-7149). The video catalogue can be accessed online.

MODERN DANCE, The Founders and the Historic Generation

Charles Weidman: On His Own, 60 minutes, Dance Horizons Video, 1990, videocassette. Narrated by Alwin Nikolais. A lovingly crafted documentary that takes Weidman from Nebraska to Denishawn, and on through his partnership with Doris Humphrey and then his work on his own. Includes actual footage of Weidman performing with Humphrey as well as Weidman talking about his work and teaching.

The Dance Works of Doris Humphrey, a two-part video documenting work of this important dance pioneer.

- Part I: *With My Red Fires* and *New Dance*, 60 min., Dance Horizons Video, 1989, videocassette. Performed by the American Dance Festival Company, these two dances from the mid-1930s deal respectively with conflict between the sexes, and conflict between the individual and the group.

- Part II: *Ritmo Jondo* and *Day On Earth*, 40 minutes, Dance Horizons Video, 1999, videocassette. Danced by the José Limón Dance Company, which performs the Humphrey choreography to this day not as historic survival but as living dance.

Denishawn: Birth of Modern Dance, 40 min., Kultur Video, 1988, videocassette. Contains historic film as well as recent reconstructions. Performed by Center City Collective, a dance troupe dedicated to the preservation of Denishawn material.

Denishawn Dances On!, 100 min., Kultur Video, 2002, videocassette. Performed by Denishawn Repertory Dancers, largest recreation of Denishawn material in existence. Pulled together by Barton Mumaw, member of Denishawn in its last year, and Jane Sherman, last living member of the original company. 23 dances.

Martha Graham Dance Company, 60 min., WNET/Dance in America Production, 1998. This 1976 television broadcast was choreographed by and produced under Martha Graham herself. Dancers include Janet Eilber, Yuriko Kimura and others from one of Graham's finest group of dancers.

Martha Graham in Performance, 93 min., Kultur Video, 1988, videocassette. Graham narrates and introduces her company performing three important works, including *Night Journey* with Graham cast as Jocasta and Paul Taylor as Tiresius.

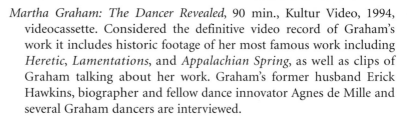

Martha Graham: The Dancer Revealed, 90 min., Kultur Video, 1994, videocassette. Considered the definitive video record of Graham's work it includes historic footage of her most famous work including *Heretic, Lamentations,* and *Appalachian Spring,* as well as clips of Graham talking about her work. Graham's former husband Erick Hawkins, biographer and fellow dance innovator Agnes de Mille and several Graham dancers are interviewed.

Mary Wigman: 1886-1973 "When Fire Dances Between Two Poles," 41 min., Dance Horizons Video, 1990, videocassette. Famous German Expressionist dance innovator, Wigman discusses her work (English voiceover.) Film includes rare footage of Wigman's last performance in 1942.

MODERN DANCE: Reformers

Cage/Cunningham, 95 min., Kultur Video, 1991, videocassette. A collage of interviews and excerpts from the work of the important partnership of choreographer Merce Cunningham and composer John Cage. Dancer Rudolf Nureyev and painter Robert Rauschenberg are among fellow artists included.

A Lifetime of Dance with Merce Cunningham and His Dance Company, 90 min., Winstar Home Entertainment, 2000, videocassette. New and archival performance film. A co-production of Thirteen/WNET New York and BBC.

Paul Taylor Dance Company: Esplanade/Runes, 58 min., WNET/Dance in America, 1998, videocassette. Performed by Paul Taylor and company and recorded in 1977. Part of the PBS "Dance in America" series.

Paul Taylor: Dancemaker, 98 min., Artistic License, 1998, videocassette. Nominated for an Academy Award in 1999 for Short Subject. One of the best dance documentaries ever made and certainly an unusually good dance video; candid, biographical and inspiring, *Dancemaker* follows Taylor's entire career.

Points in Space, 55 minutes, Kultur Video, 1986, videocassette. Featuring Cunningham Dance Company. Interviews, behind-the-scenes footage as well as performance.

The World of Alwin Nikolais, Pro Arts International, 1996, videocassette. Directed and narrated by Murray Louis. Performed by Murray Louis and dancers, *The World of Alwin Nikolais* is a five-part series which duplicates Nikolais' original stage presentations. Each part is approximately 40 minutes long, and they can be purchased separately or as a set.

MODERN DANCE: Fusion

Baryshnikov Dances Sinatra and More, 60 min., Kultur Video, 1985, videocassette. Baryshnikov, Tharp and American Ballet Theatre dancers peform including the epoch-making *Push Comes to Shove* as well as *The Little Ballet* and *Sinatra Suite*. Originally part of the PBS "Dance in America" Series.

Four By Ailey, 140 min., Kultur Video, 1986, videocassette. Performed by the Alvin Ailey American Dance Theatre. An important record of Ailey's masterpiece *Revelations* as well as other major danccs.

Pilobolus Dance Theatre, 59 min., WNET/Dance in America, 1998, videocassette. Four dances by this influential small troupe which began at Dartmouth College, part of the PBS "Dance in America" series.

A Tribute to Alvin Ailey, 120 minutes, Kultur Video, 1989, videocassette. Dance special featuring the Alvin Ailey Dance Theatre honoring its founder and introduced by dancer Judith Jamison, who succeeded Ailey as artistic director of the troupe after Ailey's death in 1989.

Alvin Ailey American Dance Theater
www.alvinailey.org

Merce Cunningham Dance
www.merce.org

Isadora Duncan Foundation for Contemporary Dance
www.isadoraduncan.org

Martha Graham Center of Contemporary Dance
www.marthagrahamdance.org

The Doris Humphrey Society
www.dorishumphrey.org

José Limón Dance Foundation
www.limon.org

Mark Morris Dance Group
www.mmdg.org

Paul Taylor Dance Company
www.ptdc.org

Twyla Tharp Dance
www.twylatharp.org

The Charles Weidman Archives
www.charlesweidman.com

Dance Magazine
www.dancemagazine.com

Dance Spirit
www.dancespirit.com

Bibliography

Anderson, Jack. *Choreography Observed.* Iowa City: University of Iowa Press, 1987.

Au, Susan. *Ballet and Modern Dance.* London: Thames and Hudson, 1988.

Banes, Sally. *Terpsichore in Sneakers, Post Modern Dance.* Boston: Houghton Mifflin, 1980.

Chujoy, Anatole. *The Dance Encyclopedia.* New York: Barnes & Co., 1949.

Cohen, Selma Jeanne, ed. *Dance as a Theater Art, Source Readings in Dance History from 1581 to the Present.* New York: Harper & Row, 1974.

Constantine, Mildred and Peter Selz, eds. *Art Nouveau, Art and Design at The Turn of the Century.* New York: Museum of Modern Art.

Crain, Debra and Judith MacKrell. *Oxford Dictionary of Dance.* Oxford: Oxford University Press, 2000.

Current, Richard Nelson and Marcia Ewing Nelson. *Loie Fuller, Goddess of Light.* Boston: Northeastern University Press, 1997.

de Mille, Agnes. *America Dances.* New York: MacMillan, 1980.

de Mille, Agnes. *Martha, The Life and Work of Martha Graham.* New York: Vintage Books, 1992.

de Mille, Agnes. *To a Young Dancer, A Handbook.* Boston: Little Brown & Co., 1962.

Denby, Edwin. *Dancers, Buildings, and People in the Street.* New York: Popular Library, 1979.

Denby, Edwin. *Looking at the Dance.* New York: Popular Library, 1968.

Duncan, Isadora. *My Life.* New York: Boni & Liveright, 1927; reprint, New York: Liveright, 1955.

Foulkes, Julia. *Modern Bodies, Dance and American Modernism from Martha Graham to Alvin Ailey.* Chapel Hill and London: University of North Carolina Press, 2002.

Fuller, Loie. *Fifteen Years of a Dancer's Life.* Boston: Small, Maynard & Co., 1913.

Graham, Martha. *Blood Memory: An Autobiography.* New York and London: Doubleday, 1991.

Jacob, Ellen. *Dancing, A Guide for the Dancer.* Reading, MA and Menlo Park, CA: Addison-Wesley Publishing Co., 1981.

Jowitt, Deborah. *The Dance in Mind.* Boston: David Godine, 1985.

Jowitt, Deborah. *Time and the Dancing Image.* New York: William Morrow, 1988.

Kirstein, Lincoln. *Dance, A Short History of Classical Theatrical Dancing.* 1935, reprint; New York: Dance Horizons, 1977.

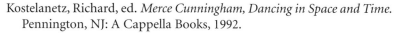

Kostelanetz, Richard, ed. *Merce Cunningham, Dancing in Space and Time*. Pennington, NJ: A Cappella Books, 1992.

Kozodoy, Ruth. *Isadora Duncan*. New York, New Haven, and Philadelphia: Chelsea House Publishers, 1988.

Kraus, Richard. *History of the Dance*. Englewood Cliffs, NJ: Prentice Hall, 1969.

Limón, José. *Unfinished Memoir*. Middletown, CT: Wesleyan University Press, 1998.

Martin, John. *The Modern Dance*. 1933, reprint; New York: Dance Horizons, 1965.

McDonagh, Don. *Complete Guide to Modern Dance*. New York: Popular Library, 1977.

McDonagh, Don. *The Rise and Fall and Rise of Modern Dance*. New York: Mentor Book, 1970.

Maynard, Olga. *American Modern Dancers, The Pioneers*. Boston: Little Brown & Co., 1969.

Penrod, James and Janice Gudde Plastino. *The Dancer Prepares, Modern Dance for Beginners*. fourth ed. Palo Alto, CA: Mayfield Publishers, 1992.

Reynolds, Nancy and Susan Reimer-Torn. *Dance Classics*. 1980, reprint; Chicago: A Cappella Books, 1991.

Robertson, Allen and Donald Hutera. *The Dance Handbook*. Boston: G. K. Hall, 1988.

Rogosin, Elinor. *The Dance Makers, Conversations with American Choreographers*. New York: Walker & Co., 1980.

St. Denis, Ruth. *An Unfinished Life*. New York & London, Harper & Bros, 1939.

Seroff, Victor. *The Real Isadora*. New York: The Dial Press, 1971.

Shelton, Suzanne. *Divine Dancer, A Biography of Ruth St. Denis*. New York: Doubleday, 1981.

Sherman, Jane Denishawn: *The Enduring Influence*. Boston: Twayne Publishers, 1983.

Sorell, Walter. *The Dance has Many Faces*. Cleveland and New York: World Publishing Co., 1951.

Taylor, Paul. *Private Domain*. San Francisco: North Point Press, 1988.

Terry, Walter. *Frontiers of Dance, The Life of Martha Graham*. New York: Thomas Y. Crowell, 1975.

Tharp, Twyla. *Push Comes to Shove*. New York: Bantam Books, 1992.

Further Reading

Au, Susan. *Ballet and Modern Dance*. London: Thames and Hudson, 1988.

de Mille, Agnes. *Martha, The Life and Times of Martha Graham*. New York: Vintage Books, 1992.

Duncan, Isadora. *My Life*. New York: Liveright, 1955.

Graham, Martha. *Blood Memory: An Autobiography*. New York & London: Doubleday, 1991.

Kozodoy, Ruth. *Isadora Duncan*. New York, New Haven, and Philadelphia: Chelsea House Publishers, 1988.

Limón, José. *An Unfinished Memoir*. Middletown, CT: Wesleyan University Press, 1998.

Shelton, Suzanne. *Divine Dancer, A Biography of Ruth St. Denis*. New York: Doubleday, 1981.

Taylor, Paul. *Private Domain*. San Francisco: North Point Press, 1988.

Tharp, Twyla. *Push Comes to Shove*. New York: Bantam Books, 1992.

Notes

Chapter One: The Precursors

1 Isadora Duncan. *My Life*. (New York: Boni & Liveright, 1927; reprint, Liveright, 1955). 3.

2 Selz, Peter and Mildred Constantine, eds. *Art Nouveau, Art and Design at the Turn of the Century*. (New York: Museum of Modern Art, 1975). 62.

3 Fuller, Loie. *Fifteen Years of a Dancer's Life*. (Boston: Small, Maynard & Co., 1913). 127.

4 Duncan. op. cit., 95.

5 Kirstein, Lincoln. *Dance a Short History of Classical Theatrical Dancing*. (1935; reprint, New York: Dance Horizons, 1977). 268.

6 Duncan. op. cit., 21.

7 Ibid., 3.

8 Agnes de Mille. *America Dances*. (New York: MacMillan, 1980). 46.

9 Sorell, Walter. *The Dance has Many Faces*. (Cleveland and New York: World Publishing, 1951). 14.

Chapter Two: Denishawn

10 Ibid., 15.

11 Agnes de Mille. *Martha, The Life and Work of Martha Graham*. (New York: Vintage Books, 1992). 41.

12 Jane Sherman. *Denishawn: the Enduring Influence*. (Boston: Twayne Publishers, 1983). 17.

13 Ibid., 11.

14 de Mille. op. cit., 52.

15 de Mille. op. cit., 54.

16 Ruth St. Denis. *An Unfinished Life*. (New York & London: Harper & Bros., 1939). 189.

17 Ibid., 191.

18 Sherman. op. cit., 63.

19 de Mille. op. cit., 68.

20 Martha Graham. *Blood Memory: An Autobiography*. (New York and London: Doubleday, 1991). 91.

Chapter Three: Historic Dance

21 Graham. op. cit., 6.

22 Ibid., 103.

23 Walter Terry. *Frontiers of Dance, The Life of Martha Graham*. (New York: Thomas Crowell, 1975). 40.

24 Graham. op. cit., 68.

25 Ibid., 106.

26 Terry. op. cit., 49.

27 Graham. op., cit., 110.

28 Terry. op. cit., 59–60.

29 Graham. op. cit., 114.

30 Ibid.

31 Ibid.

32 Ibid.

33 Graham. op. cit., 117.

34 Olga Maynard. *American Modern Dance, The Pioneers*. (Boston: Little Brown & Co., 1969). 127.

35 Ibid., 130.

36 Ibid., 131.

37 de Mille. op. cit., 102.

38 Maynard. op. cit., 143.

39 Elinor Rogisin. *The Dance Makers, Conversations with American Choreographers* (New York: Walker & Co., 1980). 16.

40 Sherman. op. cit., 41.

41 Terry, op. cit., 73.

42 José Limón. *An Unfinished Memoir*. (Middletown, CT: Wesleyan University Press, 1998). 32.

43 Terry. op. cit., 62.

Chapter Four: The Reformers and Post-Modern Dance

44 Kostelantz, Richard, ed. *Merce Cunningham, Dancing in Space and Time*. (Pennington, NJ: A Cappella Books, 1992). 39.

45 Edwin Denby. "Elegance in Isolation." *Looking at the Dance*. (New York: Popular Library, 1968). 303–304.

46 Deborah Jowitt. *The Dance in Mind*. (Boston: David Godine, 1985). 199.

47 Paul Taylor. *Private Domain*. (San Francisco: North Point Press, 1988). 80.

Notes

Chapter Five: Fusion

48 Twyla Tharp. *Push Comes to Shove.* (New York: Bantam Books). 3.

49 Graham. op. cit., 69.

50 Taylor. op. cit., 94.

51 Ibid., 30.

52 Ibid., 47–48.

53 Ibid., 54.

54 Taylor. op. cit., 161.

55 Tharp. op. cit., 89.

56 Don McDonagh. *The Rise and Fall of Modern Dance.* (New York: Mentor Book, 1970). 109.

57 Tharp. op. cit., 88–89.

58 Ibid., 177–178.

59 Ibid., 185–186.

60 Ibid., 205.

61 Ibid.

62 Ibid., 218.

63 Jowitt. op. cit., 336.

A Modern Dance Class

64 Agnes de Mille. *To A Young Dancer, A Handbook.* (Boston: Little Brown & Co. 1962). 12.

Abstract Expressionism, 60
Ag'ya, L', 57
Ailey, Alvin, 57, 65, 89
Alcestis, 62
American Ballet Theatre, 75-78, 79
American Indian myth, and Shawn, 34
Annie Get Your Gun, 56
Appalachian Spring, 52-53, 58, 70
Artistic dance, 38
Art Nouveau, 15-16
As Time Goes By, 75

Balanchine, George, 39
    and *Episodes,* 68-71
    and School of American Ballet, 72
    and Tharp, 72
Ballet
    and experimenters, 54, 65
    and fusion with modern dance, 68-83
    in modern dance class, 91
Barre, in modern dance class, 87
Baryshnikov, Mikhail, 75-78, 79, 82
Bennington College Dance Festival, 48-51, 56
Beyer, Hilda, 25
Birth of a Nation (film), 32
Black dance
    and Ailey, 57, 65-66, 89
    and Dunham, 57
    and Horton, 57, 65, 86, 89
    and Primus, 57
    and Tamiris, 47-48, 56
BodyVox, 79
Breathing technique, and Graham, 42
Brice, Fanny, 34

Brooks, Louise, 32
Brown, Trisha, 64

Cabaret, 55
Cage, John
    and Cunningham, 58, 59
    and Taylor, 62
Camelot, 56
Castle, Irene and Vernon, 23
Chicago, 55
Childs, Lucinda, 64
Civil Rights Movement, 63
Clair de Lune, 42
Clytemnestra, 62
Cobras, 29
Colleges/universities, dance programs in, 48-51, 56, 79
Colorado College, summer dance institute at, 56
Company of Male Dancers, 36, 49
Contact improvisation, 79
Contraction and a release, 42
Copeland, Aaron, and *Appalachian Spring,* 52-53, 70
Creative Dance, as introductory course on modern movement, 86
Crowsnest, 79
Cunningham, Merce, 58-60, 62, 63, 64, 65, 67, 83
    and Graham, 52-53, 89
    and modern dance instruction, 86, 89
    and Morris, 81
    and Tharp, 72

Dalcroze, Emile Jacques-, 15, 19-20
Dance Boom (Dance Explosion), 78-81
Dance Magazine, 91-92
Dance Repertory Theater, 47-48, 56

Index

Dance Spirit (magazine), 92

Dance theater, and Nikolais, 60

Dance Touring program, 78, 81

Danse Americaine, 47

Dartmouth College, dance
  programs at, 79

Dean, Laura, 64, 81

Delsarte method, 27

de Mille, Agnes, 19, 26, 35, 38,
  46

de Mille, Cecil B., 32

Denby, Edwin, 58

Denishawn, 23, 24-37
  and beginning of modern
    dance, 28
  branches of, 27
  defectors from, 35, 40, 44, 48
  end of, 36-37
  goal of, 27
  and Graham, 28, 35, 40, 41, 42
  and Horst, 28, 35, 40
  and Humphrey, 28, 35, 40, 45
  legacy of, 23, 36, 37
  methods of, 27-28
  and movie industry, 32
  and Orient tour, 34, 35, 38
  and origin of name, 25-26
  and productions, 29-32, 47
  as Ruth St. Denis School of
    Dancing, 26
  and St. Denis/Shawn duets,
    31-32
  and St. Denis solos, 29-31
  and Shawn as choreographer,
    34, 47
  and Shawn solos, 31
  tensions in, 34-36
  and U.S. tours, 28-32, 33-34,
    36, 38, 46-47
  and vaudeville, 29, 32, 33-34
  and Weidman, 28, 35, 40, 46-47,
    48

Deuce Coupe, 74-75, 81

Diaghilev, Serge, 38

Duet, 62

Duncan, Isadora, 14, 18-21, 23,
    28, 54-55, 86
  and autobiography, 21
  and Berlin tour, 19-20
  as Communist, 20, 38
  costume of, 19, 38
  death of, 20-21
  and early years, 18-19
  and Fuller, 16, 19
  legacy of, 19, 21, 38
  and movement springing out
    of emotion, 18-20, 21
  in Paris, 19, 20
  and personal life, 18, 20
  and St. Denis, 31
  and school in Berlin, 20
  and school in Russia, 20
  and skirt dancing, 18
  and Wigman, 50

Dunham, Katherine, 57

Eastman School of Music, 41

Egypta, 27

Epic, 62, 63

Episodes, 68-71

Esplanade, 63

Eurythmics, 15, 19-20, 86

Expressionism, 50, 56, 60

Expressive Movement, as
    introductory course on
    modern movement, 86

Fairbanks, Douglas, 32

Fancy Free, 77

Federal Dance Project, 56, 57

Feld, Eliot, 81

Field, Chair and Mountain,
    79

Florentine Madonna, 42

Folies Bergère, 15

Forti, Simone, 64

Forty-Eighth Street Theater,
    Graham's first solo concert at,
    37, 41-42
Fosse, Bob, 55, 56, 72
France, Anatole, 16
Frankfurt Ballet, 79
Fuller, Loie, 12-16, 18, 23, 28
    death of, 16
    and Duncan, 16, 19
    and early years, 14
    legacy of, 16, 18
    at Paris Exposition, 12-14, 15,
        16, 18
    and St. Denis, 16
    and skirt dancing, 12-16, 18

Garden of Kama, The, 30-31
Germany
    Duncan in, 19
    and Expressionism, 50, 56, 60
    and Hitler, 40, 50
    and Wigman, 50-51, 60, 86
Gordon, David, 64-65, 79
Graham, Martha, 40-41, 54-55,
    67, 82
    and awards and honors, 45, 67
    and Bennington College Dance
        Festival, 50
    and dance innovations, 40, 42-
        43, 45, 70, 88-89
    and Dance Repertory Theater,
        47-48
    and dances, 42, 43, 52-53, 58,
        62, 68-71
    death of, 45
    at Denishawn, 28, 41, 42
    and departure from Denishawn,
        35, 40
    at Eastman School of Music, 41
    and *Episodes,* 68-71
    and female dance company, 44
    and first concert dance for
        company of dancers, 43

and first solo concert, 37, 41-42
and first star turn, 34
and Hawkins, 52
and Hill, 48
and male members in dance
    company, 52, 58, 62
and modern dance as art form,
    37, 52-54, 56, 67
and modern dance instruction,
    86, 88-89
and Morris, 81
and Parsons, 78
personality of, 44-45, 71
and retirement, 55
and St. Denis, 41
and Shawn, 34, 35, 41
as showgirl, 40
and Taylor, 62
and Tharp, 72
Great Depression, 40
    and Bennington College Dance
        Festival, 50
    and Denishawn, 35
    and Federal Dance Project, 56,
        57
Greenwich Village Follies, 40
Griffiths, D.W., 32

Hair, 81
Halprin, Anna, 90
Hard Nut, The, 82
Hawkins, Erick, 52-53
Heretic, 43
Hill, Martha, 48
Holm, Hanya, 50, 56, 60
Horst, Louis
    at Denishawn, 28
    and departure from Denishawn,
        35, 40
    and Eastman School of Music,
        41
    and Taylor, 62
Horton, Lester, 57, 65, 86, 89

Index

How Long Brethren?, 56
Humphrey, Doris, 40, 44-46
  and Bennington College Dance
    Festival, 50
  and Dance Repertory Theater,
    47-48
  and dances, 46
  death of, 46
  at Denishawn, 28, 35, 40, 45,
    48
  and departure from Denishawn,
    35, 40, 44
  and first performance by
    modern dance company, 37
  and Humphry-Weidman dance
    company, 44, 55
  legacy of, 45, 46
  and Limón, 45, 46, 55, 90
  and methodology to compose
    dance, 45, 46, 47
  and modern dance as art form,
    37, 53-54, 56
  and modern dance instruction,
    86, 89-90
  personality of, 44-45, 46
  and retirement, 55
  and St. Denis, 45
  as teacher, 45, 46
Humphrey-Weidman Group, 44,
  47, 55
Humphrey-Weidman Studio, and
  Cunningham and Cage concert,
  58

Intolerance (film), 32
ISO, 79
Italy, and Mussolini, 40

Jacob's Pillow, 36-37, 49
Joffrey, Robert, 74-75
Joffrey Ballet Company, 74-75, 81
Johnston, Julianne, 32
José Limón Dance Company, 55

Judson Dance Company, 79, 80,
  89
Judson Dance Theatre (Judson
  Group), 63-65, 71, 72, 73-74

Kennedy, John F., 63
King, Martin Luther, 63
Kiss Me Kate, 56

Lamentation, 43
Legion d'Honneur, and Cunningham, 67
Letter to the World, 58
Life of the Bee, 46
Limón, José, 90
  dance company of, 55
  and Graham, 48
  and Humphrey, 45, 46, 55
  and modern dance instruction,
    86, 89-90
Limón-Humphrey, and modern
  dance instruction, 86, 89-90
Lubovitch, Lar, 81

Mamoulian, Rouben, 41
Masks, Props, and Mobiles, 60-61
Midwestern colleges, dance
  program at, 48
Mirrors, in modern dance class,
  87
Modern dance class, 84-93
  and ballet, 91
  and barre, 87
  and etiquette, 86-87
  and instructor, 87
  and introductory classes, 86
  and magazines about dance,
    91-92
  and mirrors, 87
  and music, 87
  selection of, 88
  and tap, 91
  and techniques, 86, 88-90

Momix, 79
Monk, Meredith, 64
Morris, Mark, 80-83, 88
My Fair Lady, 56

National Endowment for the Arts,
    and Dance Touring program,
    78, 81
National Medal of Arts, and
    Cunningham, 67
Natural movement theory, 27
Negro Spirituals, 56
Netherlands Dance Theater, 79
New York City Ballet, and
    Episodes, 68-71
New York University, dance
    program at, 48
Nijinsky, Vaslav, 38-39
Nikolais, Alwin, 56, 60-61, 63,
    65, 79, 89
Non Score (Cage), 62
Nureyev, Rudolf, 75-76
Nutcracker, and Morris, 82

*One Thousand and One Night
    Stands* (Shawn), 35
Orient
    and Denishawn tour, 34, 35, 38
    and St. Denis, 21, 23, 27, 29-32

Palace (New York), Denishawn at,
    34
Panama California Exposition
    (San Diego), Denishawn in,
    32
Paris
    Duncan in, 19, 20
    Fuller in, 12-16, 18
Paris Exposition of 1900, Fuller at,
    12-14, 15, 16, 18
Parsons, David, 78
Pavlova, Anna, 38
Paxton, Steve, 79

Picasso, Pablo, 39
Pilobolus, 79
Pollack, Jackson, 60
Post-Modern Dance generation,
    64-65, 72, 81-82, 89
Presidential Medal of Freedom,
    and Graham, 67
Primus, Pearl, 57
Push Came to Shove, 76-78

Radha, 21, 23, 27, 29
Rainer, Yvonne, 64
Rauschenberg, Robert, 62, 64
Re-Moves, 74
Revelations, 65-66
Revolt, 43
Robbins, Jerome, 77
Roche, Pierre, 16
Rodin, 16, 18
Roof Piece, 64
Russia, Duncan in, 20
Ruth St. Denis School of Dancing,
    26
    See also Denishawn
St. Denis, Ruth, 14, 21, 23, 77
    and dances, 21, 23, 27, 29, 37
    and dances in Oriental manner,
        21, 23, 27, 29-32
    death of, 37
    and Duncan, 31
    and early years, 21
    and Fuller seen at Paris
        Exposition, 16
    and Graham, 41
    and Humphrey, 45
    and marriage to Shawn, 25,
        34, 37
    as mother of modern dance,
        23
    and personal life, 23, 34-35
    and Ruth St. Denis School of
        Dancing, 26-27. *See also*
        Denishawn

and skirt dancing, 18
and spirit, 21, 24
and union with Shawn, 23, 24-26
and Weidman, 46-47
See also Denishawn

School of American Ballet, 72
Seven New Dances, 62
Shakers, The, 46
Shawn, Ted
and books, 35
and Company of Male Dancers, 36, 49
death of, 37
and Graham, 34, 35, 41
and homosexuality, 35
and marriage to St. Denis, 25, 34, 37
and men in serious dance, 34-35
and St. Denis, 23, 24-26. *See also* Denishawn
and summer dance festival, 36-37, 49
and Weidman, 47
and World War I, 33-34
Shearer, Sybil, 90
Sherman, Jane, 26
Skirt dancing
and Duncan, 18
and Fuller, 12-16, 18
and St. Denis, 18
Spain, civil war in, 40
Stravinsky, Igor, 39
Summer dance festival, and Jacob's Pillow, 36-37, 49

Tamiris, Helen, 47-48, 56
Tap, in modern dance class, 91
Taylor, Paul, 62-63, 65, 71, 78, 81, 83
and Graham, 89

and modern dance instruction, 86
and Tharp, 72-73
Ten Commandments, The (film), 32
Tharp, Twyla, 64, 72-78
and ballet classes, 72-73
at Barnard College, 72
and Baryshnikov, 75-78
and dances, 73-78, 81
and Joffrey, 74-75
and modern dance instruction, 86
and Morris, 81
Theatre de la Loie Fuller, Le, 12
Theatre Royal de la Monnaie (Belgium), and Morris, 82
Thief of Baghdad, The (film), 32
Three Gopi Maidens, 42
Toilers of the Soil, 31-32
Touch and Go, 56
Toulouse-Lautrec, Henri, and Fuller, 16
Trend, 56

University of California at Berkeley, Denishawn performing in Greek theatre of, 31-32

Vaudeville
and Denishawn, 29, 32, 33-34
and St. Denis, 21
Vietnam War, 63, 74

Walks and Digressions, 64
Webern, Anton Von, 70
Weidman, Charles, 40, 44-45, 46-47, 89
and Bennington College Dance Festival, 50
dance company of, 55
and Dance Repertory Theater, 47-48

death of, 55
at Denishawn, 28, 35, 40, 46-47, 48
and departure from Denishawn, 35, 40, 44
and Fosse, 55
as humorist and mime, 44, 47
and Humphrey-Weidman dance company, 44, 47, 55
and modern dance as art form, 37, 53-54, 56
personality of, 44-45
and St. Denis, 46-47
and Shawn, 47
Wigman, Mary, 50-51, 60, 86
Wilson, Sallie, 71

Works Progress Administration, 56
World War I, and Denishawn, 33-34
Worth's Family Theater and Museum, St. Denis at, 29

Xochitl, 34

Yeats, William Butler, 16
Yesenin, Sergey, 20
Yogi, 29

Ziegfeld Follies, Denishawn with, 34

Picture Credits

page:

Janet Anderson is dance critic at the *City Paper* of Philadelphia and was previously dance critic at the *Philadelphia Daily News*. She has written about dance for the *Philadelphia Inquirer, Seven Arts Magazine,* and *PBS Applause Magazine.* Prior to moving to Philadelphia, she was dance reviewer at the *Los Angeles Herald Examiner, Santa Monica Evening Outlook,* and *Long Beach Press Telegram.* She conducted and wrote Pew Charitable Trust's study on improving the quantity and quality of arts journalism. Ms. Anderson has an M.A. degree in art history from University of North Carolina at Chapel Hill. Her Ph.D. is in process at the University of Texas-Austin, (ABD). Ms. Anderson's art/dance history dissertation is on Degas and ballet images. Janet Anderson spent a year as special assistant to the chairman of the National Endowment for the Arts. Prior to that, she was legislative assistant to Senator Mark Hatfield in Washington, D.C.